quilt

quilt

Designs by
Ruth Van Haeff
and Janine Flew

MURDOCH BOOKS

contents

techniques

projects

Introduction

Patchwork quilts have been around for centuries, well-loved and well-used household items that have been treasured by each generation then passed down to the next. There is perhaps nothing more evocative of home and family than a beautiful, handmade, cosy patchwork quilt. Once painstakingly pieced and quilted by hand, such quilts can now be made much more quickly and easily with sewing machines and quick techniques such as rotary cutting and chain piecing.

Quilting does not require any advanced sewing skills; most of the quilts in this book can be made by anyone with average sewing skills, and many are suitable for beginners. All of the quilts are designed to be machine-pieced, but they can be hand-pieced if you prefer. Similarly, many of them are hand-quilted, but they can be quilted by machine if you wish. Some people love the meditative nature of hand-sewing, and don't mind taking months or years to finish a quilt; others prefer the speed and ease of machine-sewing. Neither method is better than the other; they are simply different, so choose the method that suits your lifestyle and temperament and that you enjoy the most. If you find that you like piecing but not quilting, there are commercial quilting services available; these are often advertised in the back of quilting magazines.

The quilts in this book are a mixture of traditional and contemporary designs in both patchwork and whole-cloth quilts. If you like a particular design but are not keen on the fabrics in which it has been made, remember that the choice of fabric and colour can transform a traditional design into something modern looking, and vice versa. For example, the Octagon illusion quilt (page 30) is pictured in romantic florals, but would look very striking and contemporary in zingy bright fabrics with black diamonds at the intersections of the squares.

If you are uncertain about the fabrics you intend to use for a particular quilt, buy a small amount at first and make a sample block to see if you like the effect. If not, try using the same fabrics, but arranging the components of the block in a different order. This can result in a very different effect. It is worth a little experimentation early on to avoid wasting time, money and effort on a finished quilt that doesn't meet your expectations.

Types of batting

Some battings need to be quilted closer together than others to stop them from drifting around within the quilt or fragmenting when washed. Polyester batting requires less quilting than cotton or wool batting. Some polyester battings have a tendency to 'fight' the sewing machine. Wool battings (usually actually a wool/polyester blend) provide more warmth and comfort than polyester battings. However, they require more quilting, and those that are not needle-punched tend to pill. Needle-punched wool/polyester blends are more stable and require less quilting. Traditional cotton battings require a lot of quilting, as much as every ½–3 in (13–75 mm). Needle-punched cotton battings are more stable and can be quilted up to 10 in (25 cm) apart.

giant hexagon quilt This is an alternative colourway of the design on page 38.

The parts of a quilt

Most quilts consists of three layers: the quilt top (the decorative part); the batting (the filling that gives the quilt extra warmth and also contributes to its padded look); and the quilt backing. The batting may be omitted if you want a very light quilt for summer, or if the fabrics that you have used in the quilt top and backing are heavy enough on their own. The edges of the quilt are generally finished with binding.

The quilt top

Often, a quilt top will consist of a central design or a series of blocks surrounded by one or more borders. The top of the quilt may be pieced (made of patchwork), appliquéd (with designs sewn onto a background) or whole-cloth (made entirely of one fabric). In whole-cloth quilts, the visual interest is created by the quilting alone, so these quilts are perfect for showing off a beautiful and intricate quilting pattern.

Batting

Also known as wadding, batting is the quilt's filling, or middle layer. It may be made of wool, cotton or polyester; each has different properties (see left). Cotton and wool are easier to quilt than polyester, but polyester generally gives greater loft (thickness), although not usually greater warmth.

Backing

The quilt backing is usually made of one fabric, but there is nothing to stop you from making it wholly or partly from leftover patchwork blocks or strips of different fabrics. You will normally need to join two lengths of fabric to create a backing wide enough for anything larger than a cot or lap quilt.

Binding

This is a way of finishing the raw edges of all layers of the quilt by enclosing them in a thin strip of fabric. Binding is generally made from a double thickness of fabric for extra durability, as it is the edges of a quilt that will wear most quickly. Binding is usually the last thing to be done, once the quilting is finished.

Fabric for quilts

For most quilts, it is best to use pure cotton fabrics. These wash and iron well, are easy to sew, take a crease well and do not fray excessively. Generally, all fabrics used for a quilt should be of a similar weight and weave. Using fabrics of different weights may result in some areas of the quilt wearing more quickly than others.

It is possible to use other fabrics, such as velvets, silks and satins, for a more luxurious effect. If using such fabrics, do not wash them before use. If they need ironing, do so at a low heat setting on the wrong side of the fabric. Quilts made from such fabrics should be dry cleaned, not washed.

Fabric can be solid (a uniform colour, without a print or pattern); printed; tone-on-tone (having a background printed with a design of the same colour); or checked. Printed fabrics are divided into four categories: small, medium, large and directional. Small prints may look almost like solid fabrics from a distance. Medium prints are more distinct and are often used to add visual texture. Large prints have very distinct patterns that stand out from the background. These are often used in quilts as borders or feature prints. Directional prints have a very distinct pattern that runs on one direction. Large directional prints, such as stripes, can be very effective when used in a border.

When choosing fabrics, give thought to both the balance of prints and plains as well as the tonal values of the fabrics; that is, the mixture of light, medium and dark fabrics. You will also find that the effect of a fabric may change according to the other fabrics surrounding it, with often surprising results. Experimenting with colour, tone and pattern is one of the pleasures of quilting.

Preparing fabrics

Many quilters prefer to wash, dry and iron cotton quilt fabrics before use. Wash each fabric separately in warm water with a scrap of white cotton fabric to test if the colour runs. If it does, the fabric should be discarded or used for another purpose. Otherwise, when the quilt is washed, the colour may run and ruin the quilt.

Washing pre-shrinks fabric and removes all finishes added by the manufacturer. Such finishes can make the fabric stiffer and easier to sew; if you wish to restore the stiffness, spray the fabric lightly with spray starch before sewing.

Before sewing, remove the tightly woven edges (selvages) from all fabrics; if left on and included in seams, these may cause the fabric to pucker and bunch.

Fabric grain

Fabric has three grains. The lengthwise grain runs the length of the fabric from top to bottom. The cross grain runs the width of the fabric, from selvage to selvage. The bias grain runs at a 45-degree angle to the straight of the grain.

Both the lengthwise and cross grains are straight grains. When cutting fabrics, most instructions and templates will tell you to cut on the straight of the grain. For borders, this is usually the lengthwise grain, to allow for greater length. Rotary-cut strips are usually cut on the cross grain. An arrow on the template or pattern piece shows you the direction in which the grain should run when cutting out the fabric.

Cutting fabric on the bias will cause the cut edges to stretch; this is undesirable when piecing but can be useful if you need to make the fabric curve, as when making bindings for a quilt with a curved border or when making bias strips for curved sections of appliqué.

quilting fabrics Pure cottons are best, as they are easy to cut, sew and wash.

Equipment

Not all of the items listed below are essential; some simply make the work easier. The quilts in this book are pieced by machine, but can be adapted for hand-piecing.

Sewing machine and accessories

For the projects in this book, you will need a sewing machine in good working order that is capable of straight stitch. Before you start sewing, clean out the machine's bobbin with a brush or a lint-free cloth, and oil the machine, if it needs it. Insert a new needle; a dull needle can prevent stitches from forming properly.

Sewing machine feet and needles

For piecing, you need a foot that gives you an accurate ¼ in (6 mm) seam. Most patchwork uses the imperial system rather than metric (see page 15), but most sewing machine dealers will be able to provide an accurate ¼ in (6 mm) foot. For older machines, there are feet that can be adapted. If you cannot acquire a ¼ in (6 mm) foot, place a ruler under the machine's needle and mark ¼ in (6 mm) from the needle to the right, then draw a vertical line at this point with a pen or with masking tape. Make sure the seam is accurate by sewing pieces together and then measuring the seam before starting a project.

For machine quilting, you will need a walking foot and a darning foot. A walking foot is used for all straight-line quilting. It allows layers of fabric to move through the machine without shifting. A darning foot is used to do free-motion quilting by dropping the feed dogs so that you can manoeuvre the quilt in any direction.

For general piecing, the best needle sizes to use for cotton fabrics are sizes 70/10 and 80/12. For machine quilting, use a size 75/11 quilting needle for thin and/or natural batting quilts and a size 90/14 quilting needle for quilts with high loft and/or polyester batting.

Sewing machine threads

Match the thread to the fabric when piecing; for example, when using 100 per cent cotton fabric, use 100 per cent cotton thread. If using a multicoloured fabric, use a neutral thread, such as grey or beige, to match the tone of the background. Don't use a polyester thread for a cotton fabric; over time it will cut through the fibres of the cotton. The same rule applies when choosing thread for machine quilting.

quarter-inch foot Special machine feet are available that give a precise ¼ in (6 mm) seam.

Monofilament thread, which is transparent, is the most appropriate thread for quilt tops, as it takes on the colour of any fabric that it is stitched or quilted over. Although made of nylon, monofilament thread has the elastic quality of cotton. Monofilament thread should be used as the top thread in the machine. A quilting thread that matches the backing fabric should be used in the bobbin. The top tension in the machine should be eased off so that the heavier quilting thread will anchor quilting stitches in the batting, or anchor appliqué stitches to the back.

When machine-piecing, the best stitch length is about 2.0; this should produce 12–14 stitches per inch (2.5 cm). For hand-piecing (see page 18), aim to make 10–12 stitches per inch (2.5 cm).

Rotary cutting

Rotary cutting makes it easy to cut fabrics quickly and accurately. Several layers of fabric can be cut at once.

Rotary cutters

A rotary cutter is a round, razor-sharp blade attached to a handle, protected by a sheath. Many styles of cutter are available. The standard size blade is 1¾ in (45 mm). This is suitable for most cutting tasks, but for cutting templates the most suitable blade size is 1⅛ in (28 mm). For cutting through multiple layers, a 2⅜ in (60 mm) or 2½ in (65 mm) blade gives best results. A cutter with a blade this size is also easier to hold.

Rotary cutters are held in the hand in much the same way as a knife. The handle should rest comfortably in the palm and the index finger should be placed on the top edge of the cutter handle. There is usually a ridged section in this area to help provide grip. The blade side of the cutter should face the body and cuts should be made away from the body, using a smooth, firm motion, to provide control and prevent cuts to the body.

Safety should be a priority when using the rotary cutter. The blade should be exposed only when a cut is to be made (this can be done with the thumb) and the protective sheath should be replaced as soon as the cut is finished to protect you and to prevent the blade from being damaged. Never leave rotary cutters lying about where they can be found by children or pets. A rotary cutter is essentially a circular razor blade, so treat it accordingly.

rotary cutter With blade exposed. Push the blade cover toward the blade to sheath it.

Useful bits and pieces

There are many small accessories to make patchwork and quilting easier, such as:

Erasable pencils: Used for tracing quilting designs onto the quilt top that can later be erased. Some pencils are also water soluble.

Fabric markers: Fine-tipped felt pens with an ink that vanishes automatically over time, or that can be rinsed out in cold water; test them on a scrap of fabric before using.

Quilter's quarter: A perspex rod ¼ in (6 mm) square and about 12 in (30 mm) long, used for tracing precise ¼ in (6 mm) seams along the straight edge of a template.

Seam tracers: Two connected pencils with their tips ¼ in (6 mm) apart; one is held against the edge of a template and the other is used to trace a precise ¼ in (6 mm) seam around the template.

Another type of seam tracer is a small metal disk with a hole in the centre and a groove around the outside. You put a pencil into the hole and the edge of the disk against the edge of the template, and trace around it to produce a precise ¼ in (6 mm) seam. Both types of seam tracer are particularly useful for tracing around curves.

Thimbles: There are two types, leather and metal. Leather ones are used on the fingers of the underneath hand when quilting, to prevent the needle constantly pricking the finger when it is pushed to the underside of the quilt. A metal thimble is used on the middle finger of the upper hand to push the needle through all the layers of the quilt.

Fusible interfacing: Useful for stabilizing fine or slippery fabrics, or those that fray easily, before piecing.

Rotary cutting mats

A cutting mat should be used with a rotary cutter to protect both the blade of the rotary cutter and the work surface. Rotary cutting mats are made from self-healing plastic that allows cuts to mend. The size of the cutting mat depends on the size of the work area, but the mat should be able to accommodate a quarter of the width of the fabric (approximately 11 in/28 cm). The bigger the mat, the longer the cut you will be able to make. Rotary cutting mats should be placed on a firm surface, stored flat and kept away from heat, which causes them to warp.

Rotary cutting rulers

Rotary cutting rulers (sometimes called quilters' rulers) are made of acrylic and are transparent. Designed to be used in conjunction with rotary cutters and mats, they have markings at ⅛ in (3 mm) intervals. To make the quilts in this book, you will need a 6½ x 24 in (16.5 x 60 cm) and a 6½ x 12 in (16.5 x 30 cm) ruler. The first ruler is for squaring up the fabric and cutting long lengths of fabric for borders. The smaller ruler is for cutting smaller strips of fabric.

Always measure and cut using the lines on the ruler rather than those on the cutting mat; if you cut too many times along the same lines on the mat, you will both damage the mat and erase or blur the lines, making them inaccurate.

Square rulers, which come in various sizes, are handy but not essential. The larger sizes make it possible to cut large squares in one movement. The smaller square rulers are good for cutting small pieces of fabric and for trimming up.

Accessories

Various types of pins, scissors and other accessories will make your quilt-making easier and more efficient.

Pins

Long, fine pins with heads that lie flat against the fabric are recommended, as they will go through layers of fabric easily, and allow you to sew up to and over them without the stitching puckering. Fine pins are preferable, as thick, large pins cause the fabric to bunch up and the piecing to be inaccurate. Pins should be placed at right angles to seams. For appliqué, special appliqué and sequin pins are available; they are very short (½ in/8 mm) to prevent the thread becoming caught around the appliqué pieces as you sew them down.

Scissors

You will need three types of scissors for quilt-making: a pair of fabric shears or a large pair of scissors to use exclusively to cut fabric; a pair of thread clips or small scissors to clip threads when sewing; and a pair of scissors to cut templates from plastic and paper. Don't use the same scissors for fabric and paper, as the paper will make them too blunt to cut fabric easily.

Templates and template plastic

Transparent template plastic is used to trace shapes onto fabric in much the same way as cardboard templates. The advantage of template plastic is that it is much more durable than cardboard, so it can be drawn around numerous times without the shape becoming distorted. It comes in a plain version (for freeform shapes) and a grid version (for geometric shapes).

To use template plastic to create a fabric block, trace the block template onto the plastic then, using a craft knife or paper scissors, cut it out. Template plastic can also be used for appliqué.

Commercial templates are also available. These are made of rigid plastic and come in various shapes and sizes. Their advantages are that they are durable, so they can be used over and over again, and very precisely cut for greater accuracy.

for cutting and marking Templates, template plastic, rulers, pencils and markers, craft knife.

for measuring and cutting Rotary cutter, cutting mat, quilters' rulers, scissors, pins.

for binding and quilting Markers, binding clips, thimbles, appliqué pins, safety pins, needles.

Cutting fabric

When cutting fabric, accuracy is essential so that the individual components will align exactly and the finished quilt will be the correct size. Rotary cutting is suitable for geometric shapes; curved shapes will need to be cut by hand.

Rotary-cutting strips

To prepare fabric for cutting strips using a rotary cutter, first iron the fabric flat. Fold the fabric in half along its length, and do this again, so that you have four layers. Make sure you fold on the warp threads (the threads that run down the fabric, parallel to the selvages). This may mean that the selvages do not align. Lay the folded fabric on a rotary cutter mat with the raw edge to the right if you are right-handed, to the left if you are left-handed. The folds will now be at a horizontal position. Place a quilter's ruler over the fabric, at right angles to the folds, hold it firmly in place, and trim the raw edges with a rotary cutter. Unfold the piece you have cut off and check the angle of the cut; it must be dead straight, with no kinks at the folds. If not, refold the fabric and try again until the cut is straight.

Leaving the fabric and ruler on the mat, rotate the mat 180 degrees, so that the newly trimmed edge is to the left if you are right-handed or to the right if you are left-handed. Pick up the ruler, being careful not to move the fabric. Using the vertical measurement marks on the ruler, align the required measurement with the

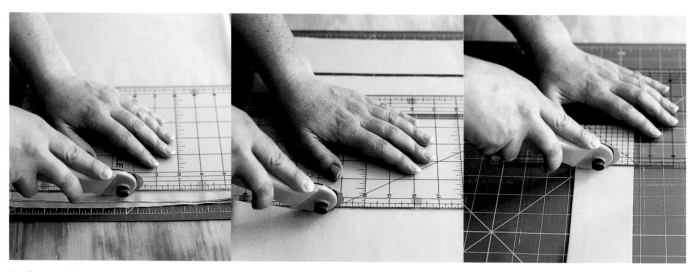

the first cut With the bulk of fabric to your left, square up the end of the fabric

cutting strips Measure by aligning the fabric with the marks on the ruler, not those on the mat.

cross-cutting A strip can be recut into smaller units such as rectangles or setting squares.

trimmed edge of the fabric. Check the measurement by placing the horizontal indicators on the ruler on the fold and the double fold. When you are sure the measurement is correct, begin cutting strips. Cut strips in batches of three or four, then turn the cutting board around to align and re-trim the cut edge of the fabric.

Rotary-cutting shapes

To save time and increase accuracy, shapes can be cut from strips. The seam allowance will need to be calculated in your measurements.

To calculate the measurement for a square, add ½ in (12 mm) for the seam allowance to the finished size of the square. To cut a square from a strip, open the strip to a double thickness only. Trim the selvage edge. Cut to the same measurement that you used to cut the strip. To check that the measurement is correct, align the 45-degree mark on the quilters' ruler with the corner edge of the strip. If it runs through the opposite diagonal corner, it is correct. Every third or fourth cut, re-align the cut edge.

To cut a rectangle from a strip, repeat the procedure for a square, remembering to add ½ in (12 mm) to the finished measurement for the seam allowance.

To cut half-square triangles from a strip, calculate the finished size of the block required and add a ⅞ inch (22 mm) seam allowance. Cut strips and then squares to this measurement. Cut once on the diagonal from corner to corner. Each square will yield 2 triangles.

A note on measurements

Measurements for patchwork and quilting are traditionally given in imperial units. This is still generally the case even in countries that have long used the metric system. Many quilting accessories, such as rotary cutting mats and quilter's rulers, give measurements only in imperial. For the quilts in this book, both metric and imperial measurements are given. When cutting, sewing and assembling the quilt, it is vital that you work in only one system of measurement. Choose metric or imperial and then stick to it; if you mix the two, your quilt will not be accurate.

half-square triangles Cut across one diagonal of a square to give half-square triangles.

quarter-square triangles Cut across both diagonals of a square to give quarter-square triangles.

To cut quarter-square triangles from a strip, calculate the finished size of the block required, and add a 1 ¼ inch (32 mm) seam allowance. Cut strips and then squares to this measurement. Cut twice on the diagonal from corner to corner. Each square will yield 4 triangles.

Cutting shapes by hand

Shapes can be cut by hand using plastic or paper templates. This method is the most practical for curved shapes, and is also the traditional way of cutting hexagons, as shown in the photographs below.

When cutting fabric using templates, the template is made to its finished size, that is, *without* seam allowances; these are added when cutting the fabric. Commercially produced plastic templates are available in various shapes and sizes, or you can make your own templates from thin cardboard or template plastic (available from craft stores).

If making a design from templates provided in a magazine or book, photocopy the template, paste it onto thin cardboard and cut it out. Always check the template's dimensions for accuracy and adjust if need be before using it to cut fabric.

Place the template on the wrong side of the fabric and trace around it. Use a sharp pencil or fine marker to give the finest line and thus the most accurate seam. This tracing line will become the seam line.

English paper piecing

This traditional English method of hand-piecing uses pieces of fabric tacked over a template of paper or thin cardboard. The pieces are then sewn together with a small whip stitch, after which the tacking stitches are cut and the paper templates removed. The templates can be re-used, but should be replaced once their edges become worn or their points lose their sharpness.

If using commercial templates with cut-out centres, as pictured at right, trace around the inner edge of the template to mark the seam line, and trace around the outer edge to mark the cutting line.

When using the English paper piecing method, mark the fabric on the right side of the fabric and sew with the right sides facing out. For all other hand-piecing, mark on the wrong side of the fabric and sew with the right sides together.

English paper piecing, step one Trace around the template onto cardboard.

English paper piecing, step two Sew tacked hexagons together to form a rosette shape.

Piecing

'Piecing' is the name given to sewing together all the separate components of a quilt. It can be done by hand or machine. To keep track of the various components, especially if making complicated blocks with many pieces, put each type of piece in its own lock-seal plastic bag and label the bag.

Machine-piecing techniques

Piecing by machine requires accurate and precise seams (see page 10). The standard seam allowance is ¼ in (6 mm). If you plan to do a lot of machine piecing, a ¼ inch sewing-machine foot will be a good invesment.

Machine-piecing is by its very nature much faster than hand-piecing, but by employing a technique called chain-piecing, you can make it even faster. To chain-piece, do not lift the presser foot and cut the thread each time you finish a seam. Instead, once you finish the seam on one unit (such as a pair of squares, as shown below), sew a little beyond the end of the seam. The reel and bobbin threads will entwine to make a 'chain'. Put another unit under the presser foot and repeat the process until you have sewn all the units. Then cut the chains between each unit and join the units to other components. Many parts of a quilt can be chain-pieced in this manner, saving both time and thread.

chain-piecing Here, pairs of squares have been chain-pieced together.

machine-piecing Machine-pieced units with seams pressed toward the darker fabric.

four-patch squares Two pairs of squares are joined to form a four-patch square.

forming rows Four-patch squares are joined to plain squares to form rows.

Fussy cutting

Sometimes you may wish to centre or make a feature of a motif. This is known as 'fussy cutting'. Use a commercial template with a cut-out centre, as pictured below, or make your own from template plastic, which is transparent. Centre the template over the motif, trace around it then cut out the shape, leaving a good ¼ in (6 mm) seam allowance.

If you want the motif to appear in exactly the same place in each fussy-cut piece, mark the edges of the template to show where they overlap with particular elements in the design, then line up these marks with the relevant parts of the printed design each time you cut a new piece of fabric.

Each block is built up unit by unit. In the example pictured on page 17, pairs of squares are first chain-pieced, then the chains are cut. Each unit is pressed with the seam toward the darker piece, then two units are sewn together to give a four-patch square. These squares are then joined to plain squares to form rows, then the rows are joined to form the quilt top. Borders may then be added.

Hand-piecing

Because it can be done much more quickly, machine-piecing has generally replaced hand-piecing. Sometimes, however — such as when sewing small hexagons or other pieces with set-in seams — hand-piecing is still the easiest way. The advantage of hand-piecing is that it is portable, so it can be done, for example, on public transport or taken on holiday with you.

If sewing using the English paper piecing method, the pieces are joined with a small whip stitch on the right side (see page 16). Otherwise, the pieces are put together with right sides facing and seam lines (not raw edges) even. Use a short, fine needle and a matching sewing thread. Begin sewing with a small backstitch, then sew along the seam line using a small running stitch. End with another small backstitch, then fasten off.

'fussy cutting' Position the template over a motif and trace around the outer edge.

seam lines The pencil lines indicate the seam lines along which the shapes are joined.

piecing Using a running stitch, join the pieces accurately along the marked lines.

Quilt layout

The quilt layout diagram provided in the pattern will show you how the various components are assembled. There are numerous ways of laying out a quilt. Blocks within a quilt top may be set square (parallel with the sides and top of the quilt) or on point (at a 45-degree angle to the tops and sides of the quilt). Blocks may be joined so that they abut one another, or be separated with sashing strips. The illustrations at right show two basic but versatile ways of laying out a quilt.

Medallion quilts have as their focal point a central panel (often elaborately pieced or appliquéd, or consisting of a feature fabric), around which there are usually several borders. These may be pieced, plain or appliquéd.

Borders may be added for decorative effect, or to increase the quilt's size, or both. Borders may have squared-off or mitred corners (see page 20).

Always refer to the layout diagram for the quilt you are making, rather than relying on a photograph. Many quilt designs, especially complex ones using more than type of block, feature optical illusions caused by the way in which the various components are combined. Sometimes the logic of the quilt's construction will not become clear until you look at the layout diagram.

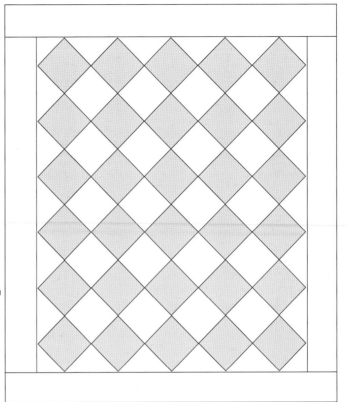

blocks on point This layout features blocks set on point (that is, on the diagonal). Setting triangles have been added to the end of each row, and corner triangles to each corner, to make the sides of the quilt square. The borders can then be added. These borders are squared off; that is, their corners are not mitred.

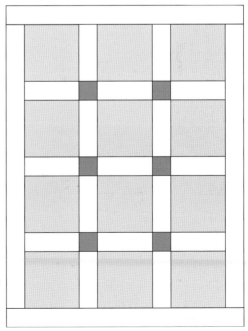

block rows and sashing rows This layout comprises blocks that are joined to narrow strips of fabric (known as sashing strips) on either side. The rows thus formed are known as block rows. They alternate with sashing rows, comprising sashing strips interposed with small squares known as setting squares. When all the rows have been joined, squared-off borders are added.

Layering a quilt

Once you have added all borders, and before you can begin quilting, you will need to assemble all three layers. This is also known as 'sandwiching' the quilt.

The batting and backing should both be about 4 in (10 cm) larger all round than the quilt top. (You may need to join two widths of lengths of fabric to obtain a large enough piece for the backing.)

Press the quilt top and backing. Lay the backing right side down on a large, flat surface, smooth it out, then tape in place using masking tape. Place the batting and quilt top, right side up, on top of it, ensuring that the top and backing are square to each other. Smooth them out. Using safety pins and starting from the centre of the quilt, pin through all three layers at intervals of about 8 in (20 cm).

If intending to machine-quilt, make sure the pins are kept away from the lines to be quilted. Once the whole quilt is safety-pinned in this manner, it can be moved.

If intending to hand-quilt, baste the whole quilt both horizontally and vertically with long hand stitches at intervals of about 6 in (15 cm), then remove the safety pins. Remove the basting stitches only once all the quilting has been completed.

Do not baste in this manner if machine-quilting, as the basting threads will get caught under the presser foot.

Adding borders

The quilt pattern will tell you what length to cut the borders to, but you should still always measure your quilt before cutting the fabric for the borders, then adjust the length of the border strips if necessary.

Measure in both directions through the middle of the quilt rather than along the edges. This is because the edges may have distorted a little during the making of the quilt, especially if any of the edge pieces are bias-cut. Use these measurements to calculate the length of each border, rermembering to add a seam allowance.

If adding squared-off borders, the side borders will be the length of the quilt top, plus seam allowance. The top and bottom borders will be the width of the quilt top with the side borders added, plus seam allowance. Sew the side borders on first, press the seams towards the border, then add the top and bottom borders. If adding more than one squared-off border, repeat this process for each border.

If adding borders with mitred corners, each border will need to be the width or length of the quilt, plus twice the width of the border to allow enough fabric for mitring, plus seam allowance. Sew each border to the edge of the quilt, beginning and ending the seam a precise ¼ in (6 mm) from the edge of the quilt. Join the fabric at the corners at a 45-degree angle. Trim excess fabric and press seam towards the border. If adding more than one mitred border, repeat for each border.

Once all the borders have been added, assemble the quilt layers (see left).

finished quilt top This quilt top has been finished with a mitred border.

Quilting

Quilting can be rudimentary, its main purpose being to hold together the layers of the quilt, or it can be decorative and sometimes extremely elaborate. Machine-quilting is quick, but nothing beats hand-quilting for sheer heirloom beauty.

Designs for hand-quilting, or elaborate designs for machine-quilting, are generally marked on the quilt top before the quilt's layers are sandwiched together. On pale fabrics, the marking is done lightly in pencil or removable marker (see page 12); on dark fabrics, use a special quilter's silver pencil. Pencil lines can be erased later. If using a removable marker, always test it on a piece of scrap fabric first.

If you intend to outline-quilt by machine, you may be able to sew straight enough lines by eye; if not, you will need to mark the quilt top first. There is no need to mark the quilt top if you intend only to machine-quilt in the ditch (see right).

Machine-quilting

You will need a walking foot for your machine; these ensure that the fabric on both top and bottom of the quilt feeds through evenly. Walking feet can be purchased at sewing machine and some craft suppliers. To avoid puckers and distortion of the quilt, machine-quilting should commence in the centre of the quilt and proceed outwards to the edges.

Find the spot to begin quilting. Bring the bobbin thread up to the surface of the quilt and machine-sew ¼ in (6 mm) of very small stitches to secure the thread and prevent the quilting from unravelling, then quilt with stitches at the normal length. When you reach ¼ in (6 mm) from the end of the quilting line, again sew with very small stitches. Clip all of the threads to the surface.

Straight or walking-foot quilting should be tackled first. Quilt from the centre point to the border edge. Then turn the quilt 90 degrees and stitch again from the centre to the border edge. Repeat for the remaining sides until you have quilted all the straight lines. Then go back and ditch-quilt or outline-quilt the blocks.

For free-motion quilting, change to a darning foot and drop the feed dogs. Follow the marked lines of your design, or stipple-quilt by moving the fabric around so that the quilting forms a random, meandering pattern.

To make the bulk of the quilt easier to manoeuvre, roll up one side of the quilt so that it fits neatly under the machine. Unroll and reroll as necessary as you proceed from one part of the design to another.

Ditch-stitching

Ditch-stitching (also known as stitching in the ditch) is the term given to quilting along a seamline. This gives a subtle effect, as the sewing is hidden in the seam. Machine ditch-stitching is quick to do, but it can be difficult to maintain an absolutely straight line. The best strategy is to sew slowly and patiently to avoid running off the track.

Because a seam is pressed in one direction, it has a high side and a low side. Quilting should be done on the low side of a seam, so that the stitching only needs to penetrate three layers instead of five.

machine-quilting Use a walking foot. This seam is being ditch-stitched.

The hand-quilting action

With your dominant hand above the quilt and the other beneath, take several running stitches at a time, making them as small and as even as you can. Push the needle through all the layers with the middle finger of your dominant hand (use a metal thimble to make this easier) and use the index finger of the underneath hand to push the needle back up to the top. Protect this finger with a leather thimble. Gently pull the stitches to indent the stitch line evenly.

To move a short distance from one part of the quilting design to another, push the tip of the needle through the batting and up at the new starting point.

When you come to the edge of the hoop, leave the thead dangling so that you can pick it up and continue working with it once you have repositioned the hoop. Work all the quilting design within the hoop before repositioning the hoop and beginning to quilt another area. If you need to quilt right up to the border edge, baste lengths of spare cotton fabric to the edge of the quilt, thus giving you enough fabric area to position the edges of the quilt under the quilting hoop.

To fasten off a length of quilting thread, make a small backstitch, splitting the thread of the previous stitch. Insert the needle into the batting and run it through the batting for about 1 in (2.5 cm). Bring the needle up to the top of the quilt and cut the thread close to the surface.

Traditionally, the best hand-quilting was considered to be that with the tiniest, most even stitches. However, longer stitches can give an attractively casual, rustic look.

Hand-quilting

Quilting by hand produces a softer line than machine-quilting, and will give an heirloom quality to quilts, especially those employing traditional designs. To quilt by hand, the fabric needs to be held in a frame (also known as a quilting hoop). Free-standing frames are available, but hand-held ones are cheaper, more portable and just as effective. One edge of a hand-held frame can be leaned against a table or bench to enable you to keep both hands free.

Hand-quilting, like machine-quilting, should commence in the centre of the quilt and proceed outwards. To commence hand-quilting, place the plain (inner) ring of the frame under the centre of the quilt. Position the other ring, with the screw, over the top of the quilt to align with the inner ring. Tighten the screw so that the fabric in the frame becomes firm, but not drum-tight.

Choose the smallest needle that you feel comfortable with and thread it with 18 in (45 cm) of matching or toning quilting thread. Knot the end of the thread and take the needle down through the quilt top into the batting, a short distance from where you want to start quilting. Tug the thread slightly so that the knot pulls through into the wadding and makes the starting point invisible. Proceed as described at left.

If you are new to hand-quilting, practise on a sample piece of quilt 'sandwich' until your action is smooth and rhythmic and produces small, even stitches. Then move on to the actual quilt.

marking the design Here, a pencil and commercial quilting stencil are being used.

hand-quilting With the fabric in a hoop, take several small running stitches at a time.

Binding

From the width of the binding fabric, cut enough 2½ in (6 cm) strips of fabric to equal the outside edge of your quilt, plus about 6 in (15 cm) to allow for mitred corners and for the ends to be folded under. Seam the strips into a continuous length, making the joins at 45-degree angles. Fold under one end of the binding strip at a 45-degree angle and press. Press the strip in half along its length.

Trim the backing and the batting so that they are even with the quilt top. Beginning at the folded end of the binding strip, pin the binding to one edge of the quilt, starting about 4 in (10 cm) in from a corner and having raw edges even. Machine-sew in place through all the layers of the quilt, using a ¼ in (6 mm) seam allowance and mitring the corners.

To mitre corners, end the seam ¼ in (6 mm) from the corner and fasten off. Fold the binding fabric up at a 45-degree angle, then fold it down so that the fold is level with the edge of the binding just sewn. Begin the next seam at the edge of the quilt and proceed as before. Repeat this process to mitre all the corners. See the diagrams at right.

When you approach the point at which the binding started, trim the excess, tuck the end of the binding under itself and stitch the rest of the seam.

Press the binding away from the quilt. Turn the binding to the back of the quilt and blind hem stitch in place by hand to finish.

diagram 1 Attach the binding, ending the first seam ¼ in (6 mm) in from the corner.

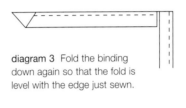

diagram 2 Fold the binding up at a 45-degree angle as shown.

diagram 3 Fold the binding down again so that the fold is level with the edge just sewn.

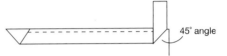

diagram 4 To end, trim excess binding, fold end under itself, and stitch the rest of the seam.

diagram 5 Fold the binding over to the back of the quilt and blind hem stitch in place by hand.

binding Fold the binding over to the back of the quilt and hold in place with binding clips.

finishing Attach the binding on the back of the quilt with small blind hem stitches.

Silk and velvet log cabin quilt

Log cabin is a classic quilt pattern that has been

a favourite for generations due to its ease

of construction and the great variety of patterns

into which its blocks can be arranged. The log

cabin block in this version begins with a 4½ in

(11 cm) centre square to which light and dark

strips — the 'logs' — are added in a spiral

fashion. This striking and luxurious interpretation

uses silks, velvets and brocade to make a very

special bedcover. No batting is used, as the

fabrics alone provide sufficient weight.

Materials

All fabrics are 45 in (112 cm) wide.
For the log cabin blocks:
   20 in (50 cm) gold brocade
   26 in (65 cm) pale pink silk
   30 in (75 cm) pale blue embroidered silk
   45 in (115 cm) mid pink velvet
   50 in (125 cm) mid blue velvet
   60 in (150 cm) burgundy silk dupion
   70 in (170 cm) navy silk dupion
   6.6 yd (6 m) fusible interfacing
For the backing and binding: 4.5 yd (4.1 m)
   mulberry heavy polyester satin
Batting at least 94 x 94 in (235 x 235 cm)
Matching sewing and quilting threads

Tools

Rotary cutter, ruler and mat
Sewing machine

Size

Approx 85 x 85 in (215 x 215 cm)

Preparation

To make these fabrics easier to handle and
   sew, fusible interfacing is applied to the
   wrong side of each to stabilize them. The
   silk dupions fray very easily; using fusible
   interfacing also helps to prevent this

Cutting instructions

All strips for the blocks are cut across the
   width of the fabric, from selvage to selvage,
   except for the navy silk dupion, which is
   cut along the length of the fabric to give
   greater economy

Seam allowance

Quarter-inch (6 mm) seam allowances are
   used throughout

preparation Iron fusible interfacing to the wrong side of each fabric.

step two Cut the end of the pale pink silk strip even with the edge of the gold brocade square.

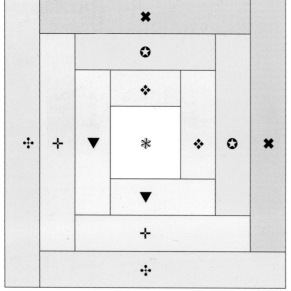

✳	gold brocade
❖	pale pink silk
▼	pale blue embroidered silk
✪	mid pink velvet
✛	mid blue velvet
✖	burgundy silk
⦂⦂	navy silk

diagram 1 block construction

CONSTRUCTION

1 From the gold brocade, cut strips 4½ in (12 cm) wide across the width of the fabric, then cross-cut to make 4½ in (12 cm) squares. From the remaining fabrics, except for the navy silk, cut 2½ in (6 cm) strips across the width of the fabric. For the navy silk, cut 2½ in (6 cm) strips down the length of the fabric.

2 With right sides facing, sew the centre square to a 2½ in (6 cm) strip of pale pink silk. Using a rotary cutter, cut the strip even with the edge of the square. Press the seam towards the pink strip.

diagram 2 Quilt construction: in this pattern, traditionally known as 'barn raising',
the squares are arranged to form alternating diamonds of pink and blue fabrics.
By arranging the blocks differently, many more patterns are possible.

step three Continue turning and adding strips as described.

block in progress The block consists of three rounds of alternating fabrics around the central square. This shows the first round completed.

3 Lay a pale pink silk strip on the unit just created. Sew, trim and press as before.

4 Continue turning and adding strips, a total of 3 in each direction, in the order shown in Diagram 1. Alternate 2 pink strips on one side of the block with 2 blue strips on the other side. Always remember to press the seams towards the new logs as each strip is added.

ASSEMBLY

5 Arrange blocks as shown in Diagram 2 (or in another arrangement, if desired) and sew into 6 rows of 6 blocks each. Join the rows to complete the quilt top.

FINISHING

6 For the binding, from the backing fabric, cut 9 strips each 2½ in (6 cm) wide across the width of the fabric. Set aside.

7 Piece backing as required and place right side down. Place the quilt top on the backing, right side up. Pin or baste the layers together. Quilt as desired: our version has been machine-quilted in the ditch along every seam. Alternatively, tie your quilt.

BINDING

8 Sew the reserved strips into a continuous length, making joins at 45-degree angles, and continue as described on page 23.

Octagon illusion quilt

Octagons are attractive shapes, but they are not easy to piece as they require set-in seams. This ingenious yet simple quilt solves the problem by using only squares. The background consists of machine-pieced large squares, with smaller squares pressed over a cardboard template then appliquéd over the intersections of the larger ones, giving the illusion of an octagon. This quilt is the perfect showcase for a subtle blending of pale, floral fabrics.

Materials

All fabrics are 100% cotton, 45 in (112 cm) wide
For the large and small squares: a total of
   3⅓ yd (3 m) assorted floral fabrics
For border 1: 16 in (40 cm)
For border 2: 48 in (120 cm)
For the backing: 3¾ yd (3.4 m)
For the binding: 20 in (50 cm)
Matching sewing and quilting threads
Batting at least 79 x 68 in (200 x 175 cm)

Tools

Rotary cutter, ruler and mat
Sewing machine
Thin cardboard
Fabric starch

Size

Approx 71 x 60 in (180 x 155 cm)

Preparation

From the thin cardboard, cut pressing
   templates C, D and E. (Cut a few of each;
   when one template becomes worn or its
   edges distorted through too much use,
   replace it with a new template)

Cutting directions

From the assorted floral fabrics:
   Cut 80 squares 6 x 6 in (15 x 15 cm)
   Cut 63 squares 3 x 3 in (7.5 x 7.5 cm)
   Cut 32 side triangles from template A
   Cut 4 corner triangles from template B

Seam allowance

Quarter-inch (6 mm) seam allowances are
   used throughout

large squares *Chain-piece pairs of large squares together.*

large squares continued *Piece pairs of squares into 8 rows of 10, pressing the seams of each row in alternate directions as shown.*

CONSTRUCTION

Refer to Diagram 3, page 36.

Large squares Arrange the 6 in (15 cm) squares in 8 rows of 10, as shown in Diagram 3, and sew into rows. Press the seams of each row in alternate directions (see Diagram 1) so that when the rows are sewn together the seams are opposing (see Diagram 2). Sew the rows together.

Small squares Spray the 3 in (7.5 cm) squares lightly with fabric starch. Place the cardboard pressing template C onto the wrong side of the fabric square. Using a dry iron, carefully ease the seam allowance over the edges of the cardboard and press well.

Remove the cardboard and position the square on point over the joins of the large squares. Appliqué in place.

Side triangles Spray the fabric triangles lightly with fabric starch. Place the cardboard pressing template D onto the wrong side of the fabric triangle, aligning the long side of the template with the base of the fabric triangle. Using a dry iron, carefully ease the seam allowance over the short sides of the template to give sharp edges and point. Remove the cardboard and position the triangles along the sides of the background squares so that their raw edges align with those of the sewn squares.

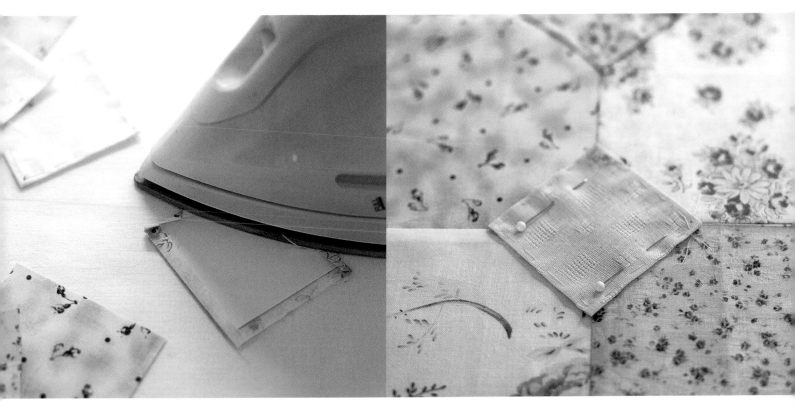

small squares Using a dry iron, carefully ease the seam allowance of the small squares over the edges of the cardboard pressing template.

small squares continued Align the pressed small squares with the intersections of the larger squares and appliqué into place.

Appliqué in place, leaving the raw edges to be sewn into the seams of Border 1.

Corner triangles Spray the fabric triangles lightly with fabric starch. Place the cardboard pressing template E onto the wrong side of the fabric triangle, aligning the 2 short sides of the template with the fabric. Using a dry iron, carefully ease the seam allowance over the long side of the cardboard only. Remove the cardboard and position the triangles so that their raw edges align with those of the corners of the quilt. Appliqué in place, leaving the raw edges to be sewn into the seams of Border 1.

Border 1 Cut 2 strips 2½ x 48½ in (6 x 123 cm). Cut 2 strips 2½ x 59½ in (6 x 152 cm). Allowing enough fabric to form the mitred corners, sew the 2 longer strips to the sides of the quilt. Press. Sew the shorter strips to the top and bottom. Press.

Border 2 Cut 2 strips 6½ x 61 in (16.5 x 155 cm). Cut 2 strips 6½ x 72 in (16.5 x 183 cm). Allowing enough fabric to form mitred corners, sew the 2 longer strips to the sides of the quilt. Press. Sew the shorter strips to the top and bottom. Press. Mitre corners as explained on page 20, beginning and ending seams a precise ¼ in (6 mm) from the outside edges. Press.

Mitred corners

When mitring corners, the additional lengths at each corner must be equal to the width of the borders. The seams must begin and end ¼ in (6 mm) from the outside edges — no more, no less.

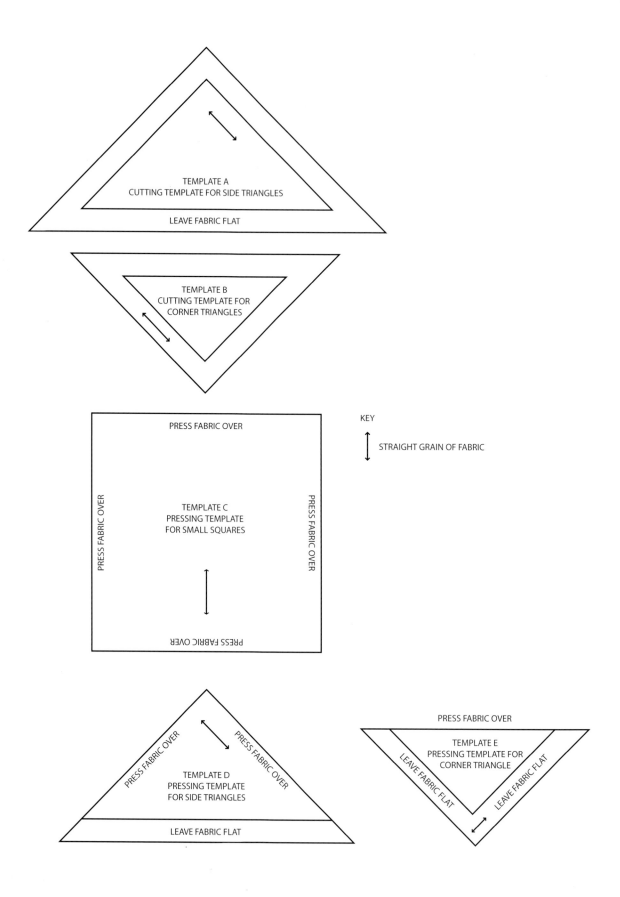

TEMPLATE A
CUTTING TEMPLATE FOR SIDE TRIANGLES

LEAVE FABRIC FLAT

TEMPLATE B
CUTTING TEMPLATE FOR
CORNER TRIANGLES

KEY

STRAIGHT GRAIN OF FABRIC

PRESS FABRIC OVER

PRESS FABRIC OVER

TEMPLATE C
PRESSING TEMPLATE
FOR SMALL SQUARES

PRESS FABRIC OVER

PRESS FABRIC OVER

PRESS FABRIC OVER

PRESS FABRIC OVER

TEMPLATE D
PRESSING TEMPLATE
FOR SIDE TRIANGLES

LEAVE FABRIC FLAT

PRESS FABRIC OVER

TEMPLATE E
PRESSING TEMPLATE FOR
CORNER TRIANGLE

LEAVE FABRIC FLAT

LEAVE FABRIC FLAT

FINISHING

Piece backing as required and place right side down. Place the batting and the quilt on top of the backing, right side up. Pin or baste the layers together. Quilt as desired: our example has been hand-quilted around the octagons, a scroll design quilted in the inner border and a cable design quilted in the outer border.

BINDING

Across the width of the binding fabric, cut 7 strips each 2½ in (6.5 cm) wide. Seam the strips into a continuous length, making joins at 45-degree angles, and continue as described on page 23.

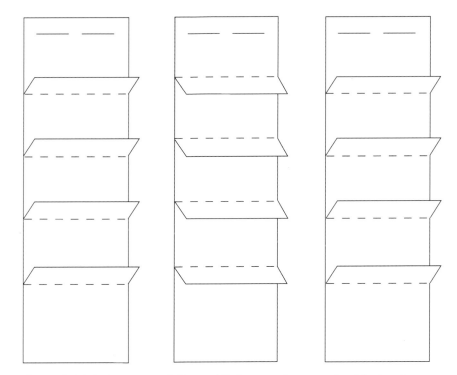

diagram 1 Join the large squares in 8 rows of 10, then press the seams of each in alternate directions as shown.

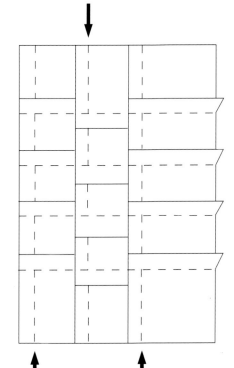

diagram 2 After being pressed as shown in Diagram 2, the rows, once sewn together, will have seams going in alternate directions (as indicated by the arrows) to reduce bulk and make the quilt top flatter.

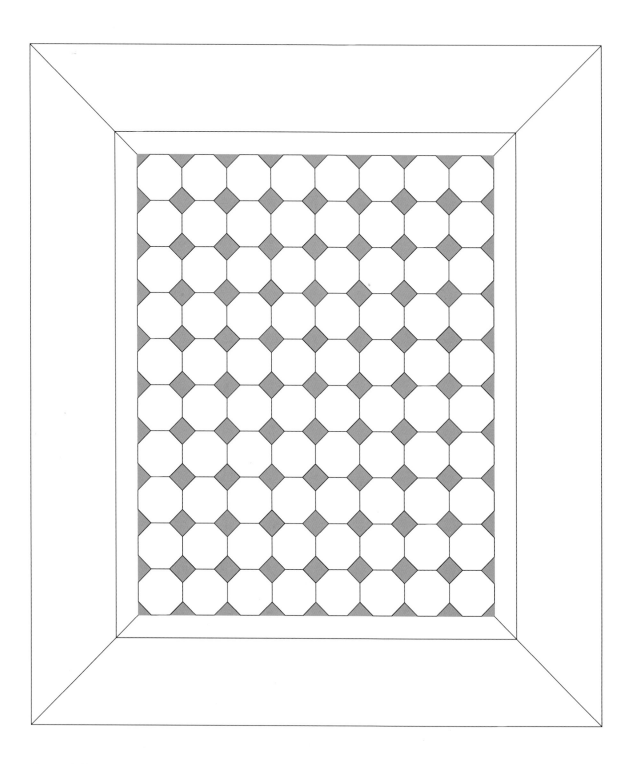

diagram 3 Quilt construction: the pieced large squares are intersected by small appliquéd squares, then surrounded by one narrow and one wide border, both with mitred corners.

Giant hexagon quilt

The hexagon is a fascinating and versatile shape that most quilters equate with the popular 'grandmother's flower garden' pattern of the 1930s, in which many small hexagons are sewn by hand into rosettes. This quilt reinterprets that traditional design by using large hexagons, machine-sewing and bold Japanese fabrics.

An alternative colourway using soft, romantic florals is pictured on pages 8 and 41, showing how the same design in different fabrics can result in a vastly different effect.

Materials

All fabrics are 100% cotton, 45 in (112 cm) wide

For the large hexagons: 19 mixed bright floral
    fabrics, at least 13 x 13 in (33 x 33 cm)

For border 1: 1.1 yd (1 m) black quilter's cotton

For border 2: 2 yd (1.8 m) bold floral fabric

For the backing: 3.3 yd (3 m) plain fabric

For the binding: 20 in (50 cm) floral fabric

Matching thread

Batting at least 76 x 64 in (195 x 160 cm)

Thin cardboard or template plastic, for
    templates for large hexagons, half hexagons,
    and quarter hexagons

Thin cardboard, for templates for small
    hexagons

Tools

Rotary cutter, ruler and mat

Sewing machine

Size

Approx 68 x 55½ in (173 x 141 cm)

Cutting directions

From the mixed bright floral fabrics, cut:

    13 large hexagons from Template A

    4 half hexagons from Template B

    4 half hexagons from Template C

    2 quarter hexagons from Template D, then
        reverse the template and cut 2 more

Seam allowance

Quarter-inch (6 mm) seam allowances are
    used throughout

preparing fabrics After cutting out the full, half and quarter hexagons, use a quilter's quarter and a pencil to mark precise ¼ in (6 mm) seam lines.

sewing Sew whole, quarter and half hexagons into rows, then machine-sew the ro
together using a set-in seam.

CONSTRUCTION

Refer to Diagram 5 (see page 45).

1 After cutting out the pieces, lay them out on a flat surface and move them about until you have achieved an arrangement that you are pleased with.

2 Sew the pieces into rows, making sure that you sew *only* from seam allowance to seam allowance, not from edge to edge. This allows for a set-in seam to be more easily made in Step 3 (see Diagram 1). Press seams open.

3 Sew the rows together with a zig-zag set-in seam, beginning and ending each seam ¼ in (6 mm) in from the edge and pivoting the needle at the end of each seam in the previous row (see Diagram 2). Press seams open.

Border 1 Cut 2 strips 5½ x 48½ in (14 x 123 cm). Cut 2 strips 5½ x 42 in (14 x 107 cm). Sew the longer strips to the sides of the quilt. Press. Sew the shorter strips to the top and the bottom of the quilt. Press.

Border 2 Cut 2 strips 7½ x 58½ in (19 x 149 cm). Cut 2 strips 7½ x 56 in (19 x 142 cm). Sew the longer strips to the sides of the quilt. Press. Sew the shorter strips to the top and the bottom of the quilt. Press.

appliquéd diamonds The diamonds appliquéd to the outer border are composed of hexagons hand-sewn using the paper piecing method.

quilting This example in an alternative colourway shows the two hexagons quilted inside each large hexagon.

Appliquéd diamonds for Border 1

These are constructed using the paper piecing method (see page 16 and Diagrams 3 and 4, page 43) and are optional.

1 From thin cardboard, cut out small hexagons using Template E.

2 Using Template E and fabrics left over from large hexagons, pin a cardboard hexagon to wrong side of fabric. Cut out fabric, adding ¼ in (6 mm) seam allowance. Cut 7 small hexagons from each of 7 fabrics.

3 Fold the edge of the fabric over and tack all round, sewing through both cardboard and fabric. With right sides together and using a whip stitch, join 7 hexagons to make a rosette (see Diagram 3). Add an extra hexagon at each end to form a diamond (see Diagram 4). Press.

Make 7 units in this way.

Three diamonds are appliquéd to one side of the inner border and 4 to the other. Spray with starch and press well. Snip the tacking thread to release the cardboard and appliqué the diamonds into place, spacing them evenly and referring to the photograph on page 42 for placement.

Template E Small hexagons for border applique design. Add ¼ in (6 mm) seam allowance when cutting fabric.

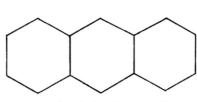

diagram 1 Sew the large hexagons into rows, beginning and ending seam ¼ in (6 mm) from edge.

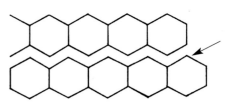

diagram 2 Sew the rows of hexagons together, using a zig-zag set-in seam.

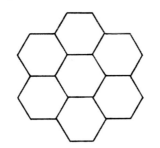

diagram 3 Hand-piece seven small hexagons into a rosette shape.

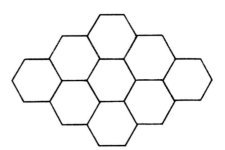

diagram 4 Add another hexagon to each end of the rosette to form a diamond shape.

FINISHING

Cut the backing fabric in half widthwise then join the two pieces together lengthwise to give a large enough backing. Place the backing right side down on a smooth surface. Place the batting and the quilt on top of the backing, right side up. Pin and baste the layers together. Quilt as desired: our example has been machine ditch-stitched along all the seams and around the appliquéd diamonds.

See the photograph on page 41 for an alternative hand-quilting suggestion.

BINDING

From width of the binding fabric, cut 6 strips each 2½ in (6.5 cm) wide. Seam the strips into a continuous length, then continue as explained on page 23.

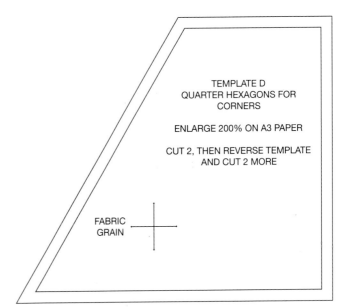

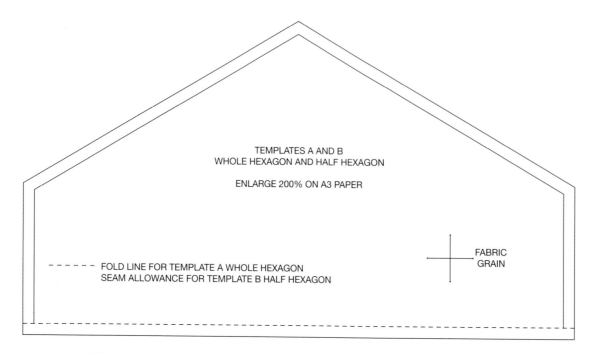

TEMPLATES A AND B
WHOLE HEXAGON AND HALF HEXAGON

ENLARGE 200% ON A3 PAPER

FABRIC
GRAIN

FOLD LINE FOR TEMPLATE A WHOLE HEXAGON
SEAM ALLOWANCE FOR TEMPLATE B HALF HEXAGON

templates A and B: whole hexagons and half hexagons For the whole hexagons (Template A), make 2 photocopies at 200% on A3 paper and join accurately along the scored line to make the full template. For the half hexagons (Template B), photocopy at 200% on A3 paper.

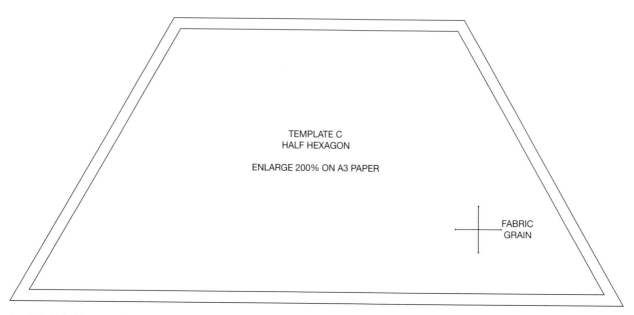

TEMPLATE C
HALF HEXAGON

ENLARGE 200% ON A3 PAPER

FABRIC
GRAIN

template C: half hexagons Photocopy at 200% on A3 paper.

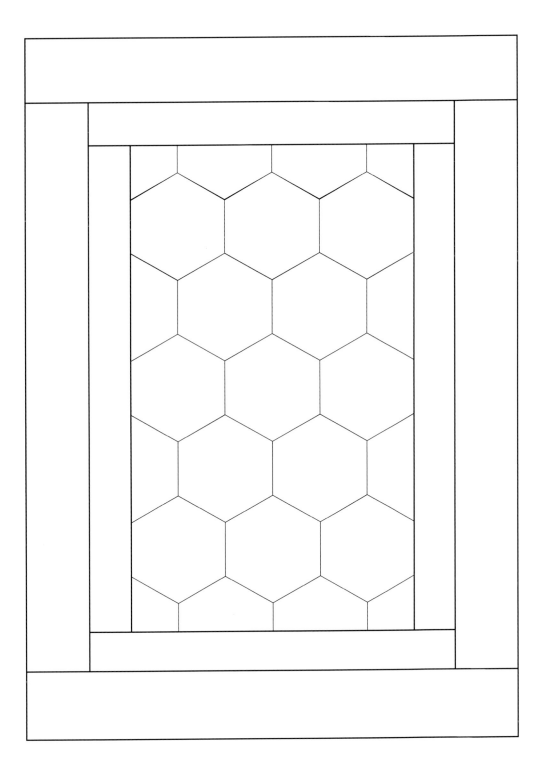

Labelling and dating quilts

Many quilters like to sign and date their quilts on the back as a record for future owners of when and by whom they were made. Signing can be done with an indelible fabric marker directly onto the quilt if the backing is a pale fabric, or on a patch of pale fabric that is then sewn onto the back of a dark quilt. An alternative is to embroider the details onto a patch of fabric and sew the patch to the back of the quilt.

A signature can be as basic as the maker and year, or if the quilt is to be a gift, you might also like to include details of the recipient and the occasion for which the quilt was made.

diagram 5 Quilt construction: full hexagons, two different half hexagons (A and B) and quarter hexagons make up the centre of the quilt, and are surrounded by two borders.

Raw-seamed denim and drill quilt

This raw-seamed quilt is a pared-back alternative to the more usual feminine quilts. It is quick to make, comprising one layer only, without batting, backing or quilting. Rather than the usual binding, the edges are zigzag stitched a little way in from the edge and the fabric frayed to give a fringed effect. The example pictured uses white thread on the right side of the quilt as a contrast, but you could use black for a more subtle effect, or a colour for a brighter look. The weight of the denim and drill fabrics makes the quilt quite sturdy and heavy even without batting and backing, but you could add either or both if you wish, then ditch-stitch the quilt to hold all the layers together and bind as usual.

Materials
All fabrics are 60 in (150 cm) wide
30 in (75 cm) grey denim for quilt top
53 in (135 cm) black cotton drill for quilt top and border
Black sewing thread
White sewing thread

Tools
Rotary cutter, ruler and mat
Sewing machine

Size
Approx 63 x 52 in (160 x 130 cm)

Cutting
From the length of the drill fabric, cut 4 strips each 6½ in (16.5 cm) wide for the borders
From the width of the remaining drill fabric, cut 31 squares each 6½ x 6½ in (16.5 x 16.5 cm)
From the denim fabric, cut 32 squares each 6½ x 6½ in (16.5 x 16.5 cm)

Seam allowance
Three-eighths inch (1 cm) seam allowances are used throughout

step one Piece together alternate denim and drill squares.

CONSTRUCTION

Refer to Diagram 2 (page 51).
Note that a ⅜ in (1 cm) seam allowance
is used throughout.

1 With wrong sides together, and using
white thread in the needle and black thread
in the bobbin, piece alternate squares of
denim and drill into 9 strips of 7 squares.
Five of the strips should begin and end with
a denim square and four with a drill square
(see Diagram 1). Press seams open.

2 Join the strips together as shown in
Diagram 2, alternating strips ending in a
denim square with those ending in a black

square to create a checkerboard effect.
Press seams open.

3 With wrong sides together, add the side
borders first. Trim ends. Add the top and
bottom borders. Trim ends.

4 Using black thread in both needle and
bobbin and a short, medium-width zigzag
stitch, zigzag around the entire outer edge
of the quilt, about ⅝ in (1.5 cm) in from the
edge. This is to reinforce the edge and to
limit the extent of the fraying. Fray the
edges of the quilt up to the stitching.

step two Join the strips to form a checkerboard-effect quilt top.

step three Machine zig-zag around the entire outer edge of the quilt, about ⅝ in (1.5 cm) in from the edge, then fray the threads up to the stitching.

make 5 rows

make 4 rows

diagram 1 Piecing squares into rows

KEY

denim

drill

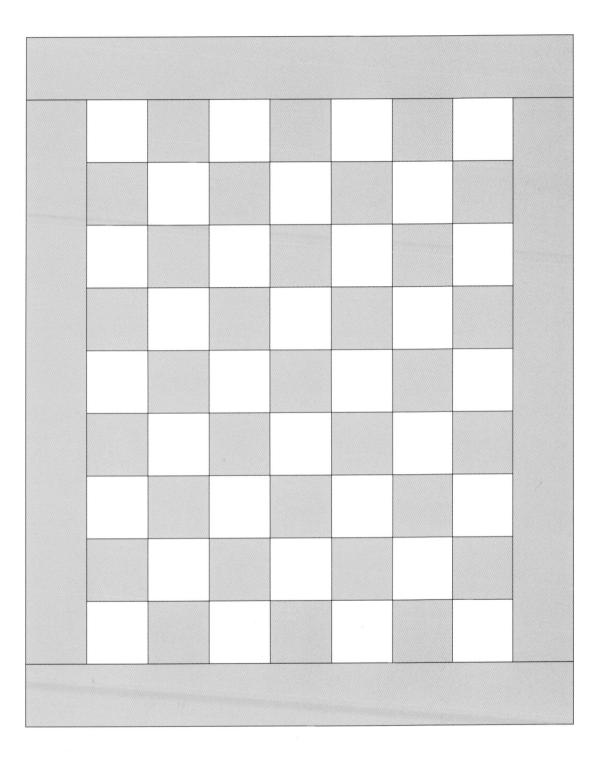

diagram 2 Quilt construction: a checkerboard pattern of black drill and grey demin squares is surrounded by a black drill border. The edges are machine zig-zagged and frayed.

1930s scrap quilt

'Waste not, want not', a motto appropriate
to the Depression-era 1930s, is the inspiration
for this scrap quilt. It uses a mix of jaunty
reproduction 1930s and 40s print fabrics, but
is suited to any small scraps of fabric. Mix them
up as you please for a fun, easy quilt.

This quilt comprises two different blocks; one
with a four-patch centre and the other with a
novelty-print centre.

Materials

All fabrics are 100% cotton, 45 in (112 cm) wide
For the blocks: a total of 2¾ yd (2.4 m) 1930s/
    40s reproduction prints (equivalent to approx
    9 fat quarters or 18 fat eighths)
    8 in (20 cm) feature print fabric
For the sashing and border 1: 36 in (90 cm)
For border 2: 40 in (100 cm)
For the binding: 20 in (50 cm)
For the backing: 3.5 yd (3.2 m)
Matching thread
Batting 78 x 67 in (200 x 170 cm)
22 assorted buttons (optional)

Tools

Rotary cutter, ruler and mat
Sewing machine

Size

Approx 70 x 59 in (180 x 150 cm)

Cutting directions

From the 1930s/40s reproduction fabrics:
    Cut 120 rectangular strips 2 x 7 in
        (5 x 17.5 cm) for Blocks A and B
    Cut 88 squares 3 x 3 in (7.5 x 7.5 cm)
        for Block B
    Cut 20 squares 2 x 2 in (5 x 5 cm) for
        the setting squares
From the feature print, cut 8 squares
    5½ x 5½ in (14 x 14 cm)
From the sashing fabric, cut 10 strips each
    2 in (5 cm) wide across the width of the
    fabric. Cross-cut into 49 pieces 2 x 8½ in
    inches (5 x 2½ cm)

Seam allowance

Quarter-inch (6 mm) seam allowances are
    used throughout

block B, step one Chain-piece pairs of 3 in (7.5 cm) squares together.

block B, step two Join pairs of squares to complete the central four-patch block.

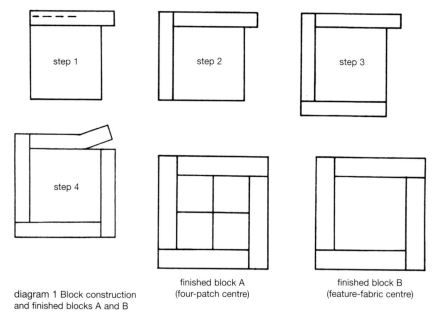

step 1

step 2

step 3

step 4

diagram 1 Block construction
and finished blocks A and B

finished block A
(four-patch centre)

finished block B
(feature-fabric centre)

CONSTRUCTION
Block A (make 8)

Finished size of the block is 8 in (21.5 cm). Each block requires 1 square 5½ x 5½ in (14 x 14 cm) and 4 rectangular strips each 2 x 7 in (5 x 17.5 cm).

1 Sew a rectangular strip to the feature-print square, sewing only part of the first seam as shown in Diagram 1. Press seam toward coloured strip.

2 Add the remaining rectangular strips as shown in Diagram 1, sewing from edge to edge and matching each end. Sew the rest of the unfinished first seam.

block B, step three Sew a rectangular strip to one edge of the four-patch block using a partial seam (end the seam 1 in/2.5 cm or so from the edge of the four-patch).

block B, step four Once all four rectangular strips have been added, the partial seam made for the first strip can be completed.

Block B (make 22)

Finished size of the block is 8 in (21.5 cm). Each block requires 4 squares each 3 x 3 in (7.5 x 7.5 cm) and 4 rectangular strips each 2 x 7 in (5 x 17.5 cm).

1 Sew the squares together in pairs.

2 Sew the pairs together to make a 5½ in (14 cm) square.

3 Sew the strips around the four-patch square in the same manner as for Block A.

4 Complete the partial first seam in the same manner as for Block A.

QUILT ASSEMBLY See Diagrams 2–5.

Sashing Rows Each row alternates 5 sashing strips and 4 setting squares, beginning and ending with a sashing strip (see Diagram 2). Sew 5 rows thus.

Block rows Each row alternates 5 blocks and 4 sashing strips, beginning and ending with a block. Arrange all the components as shown in Diagram 5, then sew the blocks and sashing strips together (see Diagrams 3 and 4). Sew 6 rows thus.
Alternate the block rows with the sashing rows, beginning and ending with a block row, to complete your quilt top (see Diagram 5).

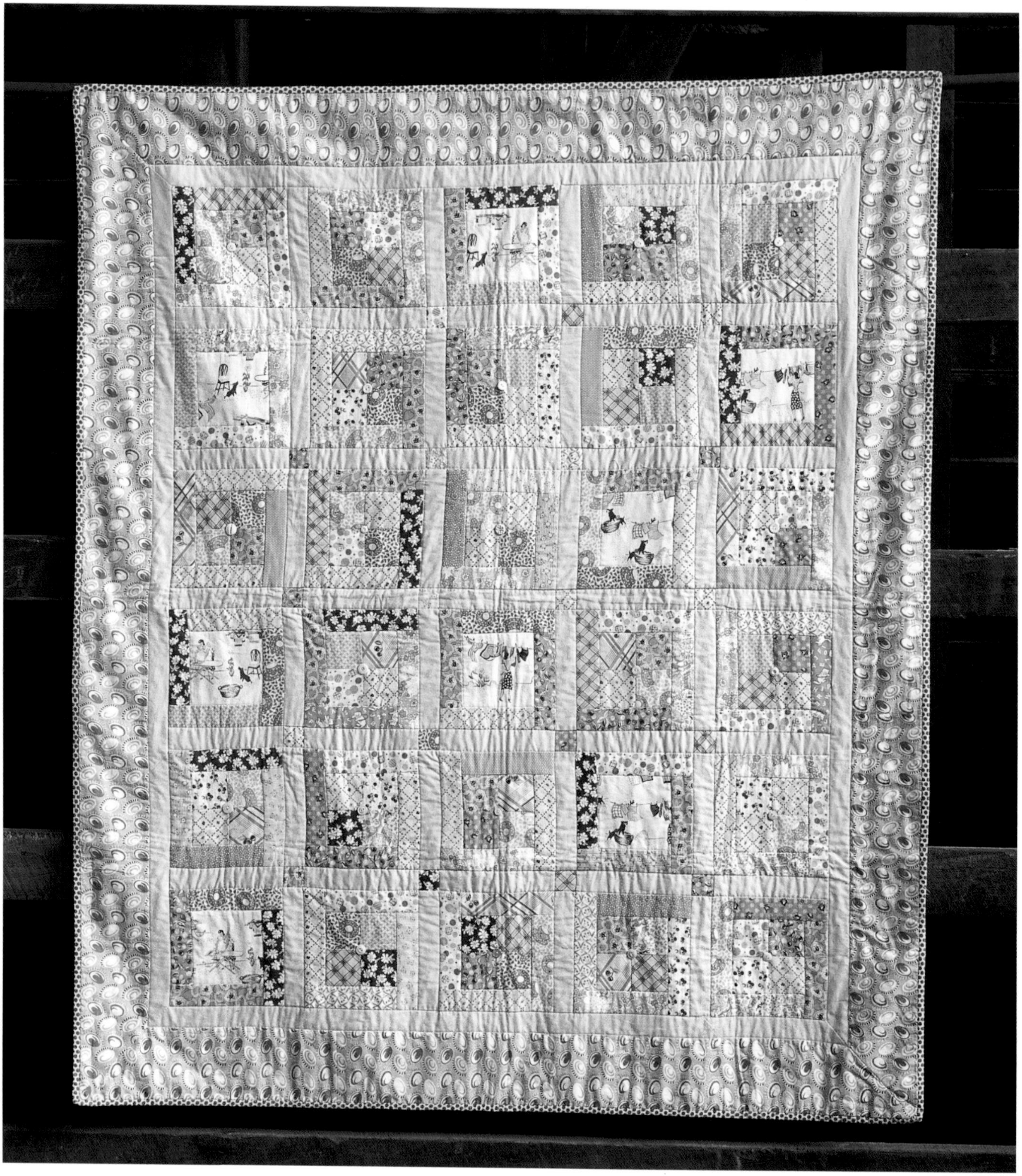

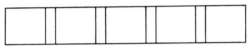

diagram 2 Sashing rows: each has 5 sashing strips and 4 setting squares.

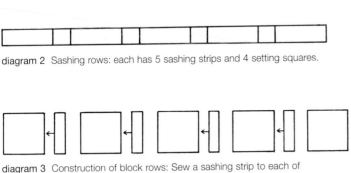

diagram 3 Construction of block rows: Sew a sashing strip to each of 4 blocks, then join them all together and add another block to the end.

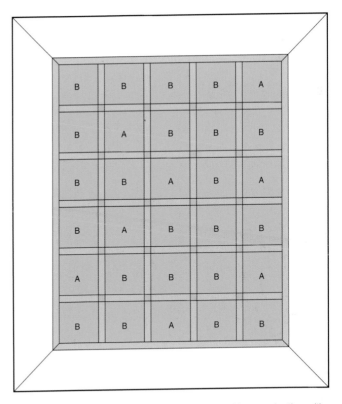

diagram 5 Quilt assembly: the blocks are separated from each other with sashing strips, and the block rows alternate with sashing rows.

diagram 4 The finished block row.

Border 1 From the sashing fabric, cut 2 strips each 2 x 56 in (5 x 142.5 cm). Cut 2 strips 2 x 49½ in (5 x 126 cm). Sew the 2 longer strips to the sides of the quilt. Press. Sew the 2 shorter strips to the top and bottom of the quilt. Press.

Border 2 Cut 2 strips each 5½ x 59 in (14 x 150 cm). Cut 2 strips each 5½ x 59½ in (14 x 151.5 cm). Sew the first 2 strips to the sides of the quilt. Press. Sew the remaining 2 strips to the top and the bottom of the quilt. Press.

FINISHING

Cut the backing fabric in half widthwise. Sew the two pieces together along the selvedges. Place the backing right side down on a flat surface. Place the batting and the quilt on top of the backing, right side up. Pin and baste the layers together. Quilt as desired: our example is machine ditch-stitched along all seams and a button sewn to the centre of each four-patch block.

BINDING

Across the width of the binding fabric, cut 7 strips each 2½ in (6.5 cm) wide. Seam the strips into a continuous length and proceed as instructed on page 23.

Pleated silk quilt

This highly textural, monochrome quilt will add a touch of luxury to any room. If you can draw and sew a straight line, you can make this; all it requires is a little patience to sew the many seams. As this quilt takes quite a lot of silk, it is rather an investment, but if you wish to cut costs, you could back it with a quilter's cotton in a matching shade rather than with the silk.

Materials

All fabrics are 45 in (112 cm) wide.

10.5 yd (9.5 m) silk dupion for the quilt top, backing and binding

OR

6.6 yd (6 m) silk dupion for the quilt top and binding

AND

4 yd (3.6 m) quilter's cotton in a matching shade for the backing and binding

Matching sewing thread

Batting at least 90 x 78 in (230 x 195 cm)

Tools

Long quilter's ruler

Tailor's chalk

Sewing machine with walking foot

Size

Approx 83 x 69 in (210 x 175 cm)

Cutting instructions

Square up the fabric.

From the silk, cut 7 strips each 2½ in (6.5 cm) wide across the width of the fabric for the binding

For the quilt top, cut two pieces of silk each 3 yd (2.7 m) long

For the backing, cut the remaining silk, or the quilter's cotton if using, into halves.

Seam allowance

Three-eighths inch (1 cm) seam allowances are used throughout

step two Rule and mark a 4¾ in (12 cm) grid on the right side of each panel of the quilt top.

step three For the vertical pleats, fold along each ruled line and sew ⅜ in (1 cm) in from the fold line.

QUILT TOP

Refer to Diagram 1.

1 Square up the top edge of the fabric. Cut off and discard ⅜ in (1 cm) along the selvedges. Machine zig-zag along the sides and top edge of fabric to prevent fraying.

2 Using tailor's chalk and a long plastic quilter's ruler, mark out and rule a 4¾ in (12 cm) square grid on the right side of both panels. Once you have ruled all the lines horizontally and vertically, cut off excess fabric at bottom of fabric, leaving ⅜ in (1 cm) seam allowance. Machine zig-zag along the bottom edge, as before, to prevent fraying.

3 Sew the vertical pleats on each panel of fabric before joining the two panels together, as this will be less unwieldy. Crease along each vertical fold line. To make the pleats, machine-sew using a medium stitch length ⅜ in (1 cm) in from the fold line.

4 Once all the pleats are sewn on each panel, join the two panels: with RS together, match raw edges and fold lines, then sew a ⅜ in (1 cm) seam. (The finished seam will be concealed in a fold line.)

5 Sew all the horizontal pleats in the same manner as for Step 3.

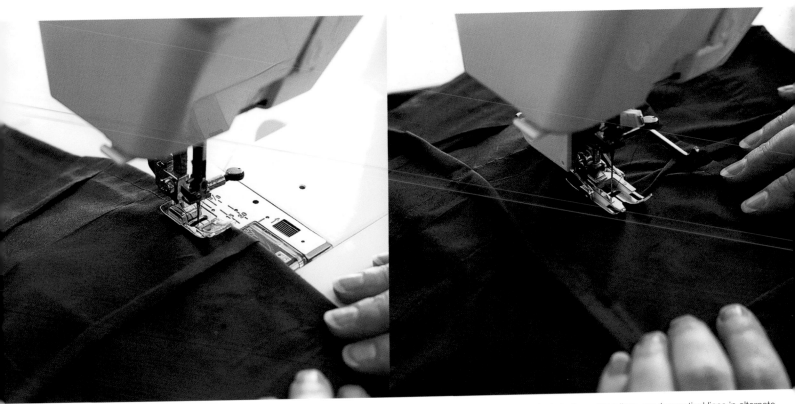

step five Sew the horizontal pleats in the same manner.

quilting Catch down the pleats in the quilting lines, sewing vertical lines in alternate directions and horizontal lines in the same direction. Use a walking foot, as shown.

FINISHING

For the backing, piece the two lengths of fabric together lengthwise. Place the backing right side down on a flat surface. Place the batting and quilt top on the backing, right side up. Pin and baste.

The pleats are caught down in the quilting lines, which are made halfway down each square of the grid. Many sewing machines have an adjustable arm that acts as a guide, allowing you to sew accurate lines by aligning the arm with a previously sewn straight line. Otherwise, rule the quilting lines, or do them freehand if you have an accurate eye.

Making sure all pleats are caught down in the correct direction, quilt the vertical lines, sewing them in alternate directions. Then quilt all the horizontal lines, sewing them in the same direction.

BINDING

Seam the reserved binding strips into a continuous length, making the joins at 45 degree angles, and proceed as described on page 23.

CARING FOR YOUR QUILT

Note that due to the nature and mixture of fabrics used, this quilt should not be washed; dry clean it instead.

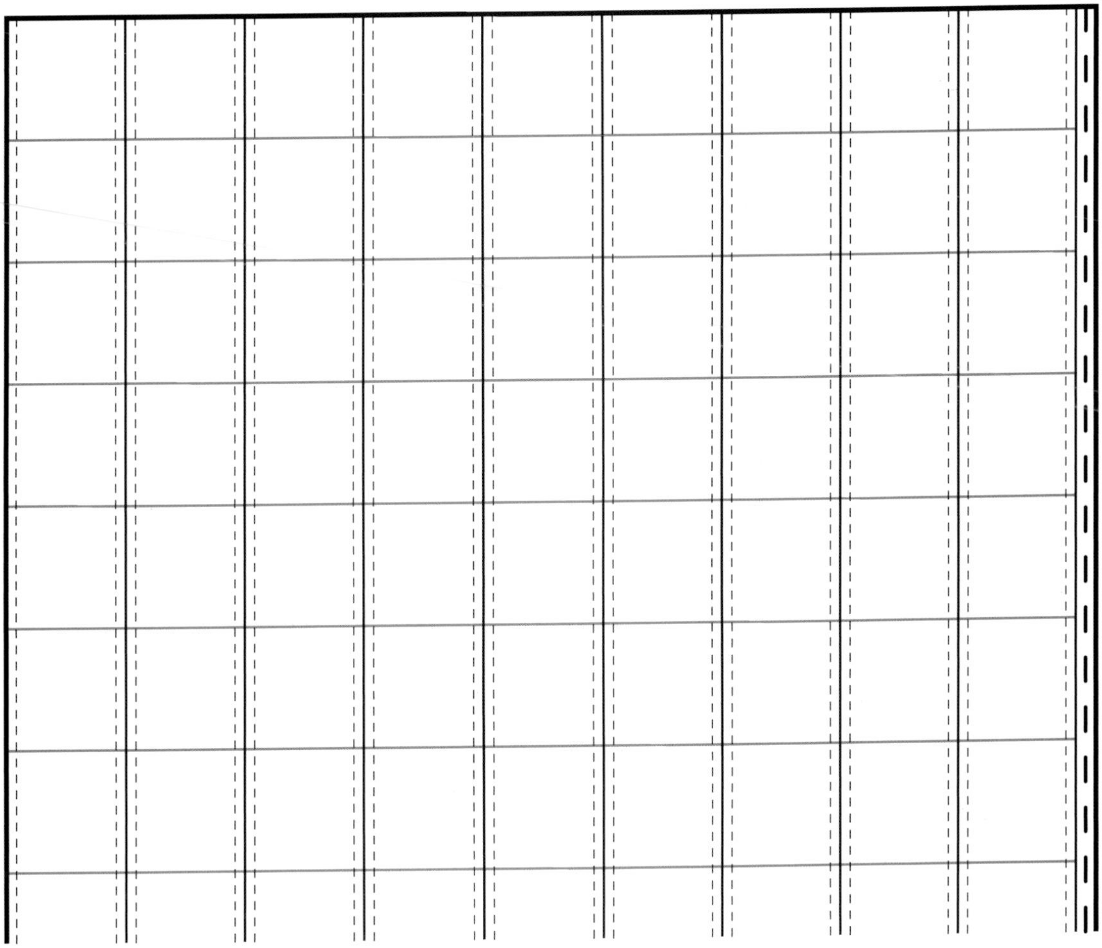

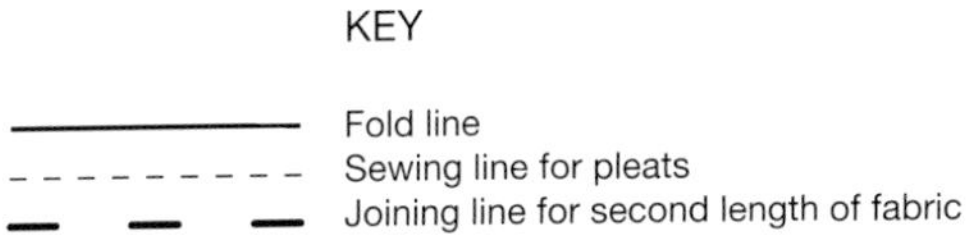

KEY

———————— Fold line
- - - - - - - Sewing line for pleats
▬ ▬ ▬ Joining line for second length of fabric

diagram 1 The quilt top consists of two panels (this diagram shows only the upper part of one of the panels). Each is marked into a 4¾ in (12 cm) grid and the vertical pleats are sewn first. The two panels are then joined and the horizontal pleats are sewn next. After the quilt 'sandwich' is made, the quilt is machine-quilted to catch down the pleats.

Square-in-a-square quilt

Beautiful Japanese fabrics are the focus of this easy-to-piece quilt, with the dark indigos forming a sharp contrast to the cream centres, and both framed with russet sashing strips and borders.

Materials

All fabrics are 100% cotton, 45 in (112 cm) wide

For the blocks:

A total of 1.9 yd (1.7 m) assorted Japanese print fabrics

A total of 16 in (40 cm) assorted cream fabrics

For the sashing, border and binding: 2.1 yd (1.9 m) russet fabric

For the backing: 3 yd (2.7 m)

Matching sewing thread

Batting at least 68 x 54 in (175 x 140 cm)

Tools

Rotary cutter, ruler and mat

Sewing machine

Size

Approx 64½ x 49½ in (163 x 125 cm)

Cutting directions

From the indigo fabrics, cut:

For the blocks:

96 strips each 3½ x 2 in (9 x 5 cm)

96 strips each 6½ x 2 in (16.5 x 5 cm)

(Note: if you want each square to have the same fabric on all sides, cut even numbers of each strip for each fabric)

For the setting squares:

35 squares 2 x 2 in (5 x 5 cm)

From the cream fabrics, cut 48 squares 3½ x 3½ in (9 x 9 cm)

From the length of the russet fabric, cut:

For the border:

2 strips 3½ x 59 in (9 x 150 cm)

2 strips 3½ x 56 in (9 x 142 cm)

For the binding: 4 strips 2½ in (6.5 cm) wide

For the sashing: from the remaining russet fabric, cut 82 strips 6½ x 2 in (16.5 x 5 cm)

Seam allowance

Quarter-inch (6 mm) seam allowances are used throughout

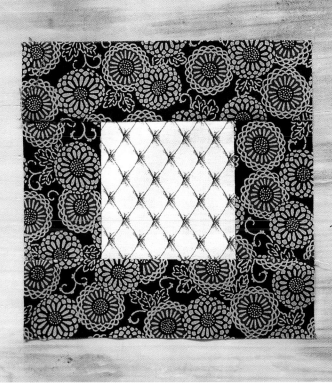

step one Sew a short indigo strip to opposite sides of a cream square.

step two Sew a longer indigo strip to the top and bottom of the unit formed in Step 1.

CONSTRUCTION OF BLOCK

1 Sew a 3½ x 2 in (9 x 5 cm) indigo strip to opposite sides of a 3½ x 3½ cream square. Press seams towards indigo strips.

2 Sew a 6½ x 2 in (16.5 x 5 cm) strip to the top and bottom of the unit formed in Step 1. Press seams towards indigo strips.

Make 48 blocks. Avoid duplicating the same print combinations too many times.

SASHING

Block rows Each block row consists of 6 blocks alternating with 5 sashing strips (see Diagram 1). Each row begins and ends with a block. On a flat surface, arrange the blocks until you have an arrangement that you are pleased with. For a neat effect, make sure that the blocks are positioned so that the long strips on each side all face the same way. Make 8 block rows.

Sashing rows Each sashing row consists of 6 sashing strips and 5 setting squares. Each row begins and ends with a sashing strip. Join the sashing strips and setting squares to make 7 rows.

Stitch the rows together, alternating block rows and sashing rows, beginning and ending with a block row. See Diagram 1.

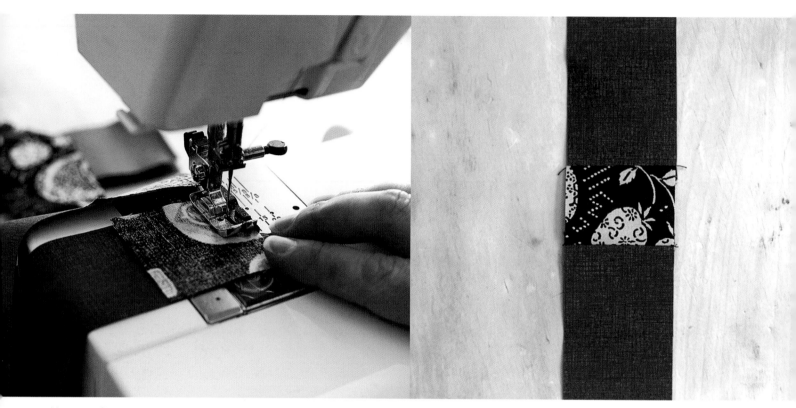

sashing rows Chain-piece indigo setting squares to russet sashing strips.

sashing rows continued Join 6 sashing strips to 5 setting squares to complete th
sashing row.

BORDER

Sew the 2 longer strips to the side of the
quilt. Press. Sew the 2 shorter strips to the
top and bottom of the quilt. Press.

FINISHING

Cut the backing fabric in half widthwise.
Join the two pieces lengthwise (along the
selvedges). Press seam open.
Place the backing right side down on a flat
surface. Place the batting and the quilt on
top of the backing, right side up. Pin and
baste the layers together. Quilt as desired:
our example is machine ditch-stitched
around the cream squares and along the
sashing rows and border seam.

BINDING

Seam the reserved binding strips into a
continuous length and proceed as described
on page 23.

diagram 1 Lay out the blocks so that the longer side strips all face in the same direction. Join the blocks to sashing strips to form the block rows, and the sashing strips to the setting squares to form the sashing rows.

Scrappy ninepatch quilt

Traditional quilt patterns often take their name

from their method of construction, as is the

case with this design, a ninepatch. Each block

consists of three rows of three squares in two

alternating colours. Despite the number of

squares involved, this is a simple project suitable

for a beginner. Quick quilting methods such as

rotary cutting and chain-piecing make it easy

to work both quickly and accurately.

Materials
All fabrics are 100% cotton, 45 in (112 cm) wide
For the cream squares, setting triangles and binding:
    4.4 yd (4 m) cream fabric
For the ninepatch squares: a total of 1.9 yd (1.7 m)
    assorted print fabrics (7 fat quarters or 14 fat eighths;
    or use fabric scraps)
For the backing: 4.1 yd (3.7 m) quilter's cotton
Matching sewing thread
Batting at least 80 x 75 in (200 x 185 cm)

Tools
Rotary cutter, ruler and mat
Sewing machine

Size
Approx 75 x 69 in (190 x 175 cm)

Cutting directions
For the ninepatch blocks:
    From the width of each print fabric, cut 5 strips
      2 in (5 cm) wide
    From the width of the cream fabric, cut the
      same total number of strips 2 in (5 cm) wide
From the cream fabric:
    For the cream background squares, cut
      7 strips 5 in (12.5 cm) wide across width of fabric.
      Cross-cut into 63 squares 5 x 5 in (12.5 x 12.5 cm)
    For the setting triangles, cut 3 strips each 7½ in
      (19 cm) wide across the width of the fabric.
      Cross-cut into 15 squares 7½ x 7½ in (19 x 19 cm).
      Recut 11 squares on both diagonals to yield 44
      triangles (of which you will use only 42); see Diagram
      2 on page 73
    For the corner triangles, cut 2 squares each 4½ x
      4½ in (11.5 x 11.5 cm) and recut on one diagonal to
      yield 4 squares; see Diagram 3 on page 73

Step one Sew a print strip to each side of a plain strip.

step one (large A and B units) A units consist of 2 print strips flanking a plain strip. B units have 2 plain strips flanking a print strip.

Binding

Cut 8 strips each 2½ in (6 cm) wide across the width of the cream fabric. Seam the strips into a continuous length, making the joins at 45-degree angles, then proceed as described on page 23.

CONSTRUCTION

In this quick ninepatch method, long strips of fabric are joined, then crosscut and the smaller units rejoined to form the block. Three different sets of strips are needed: two A units, each comprising 2 print strips flanking a cream strip, and one B unit of 2 cream strips flanking a print strip (see photograph). If you are using scrap fabrics, you will need to trim the cream strips to the same length as those of the print fabric. Refer to Diagram 1 and photograph above.

Ninepatch blocks

1 For the large A units, sew a print strip to each side of a cream strip. Press seams toward the print strip. For the large B units, sew a plain strip to each side of a print strip. Make twice as many large A units as large B units for each print.

2 Place an A unit face up on an ironing board. Place a B unit face down onto the A unit. Press together. Place a second A unit on top.

3 Carefully transfer the sets to a cutting mat and cross-cut at 2 in (5 cm) intervals (see photograph).

4 Chain-piece a small A unit to a small B unit, then add the second small A unit to

step two Layer the large A and B units on an ironing board and press.

step three Transfer the sets to a cutting mat and cross-cut at 2 in (5 cm) intervals.

the other side to complete the block. Sew 80 blocks in this manner.

5 Arrange the blocks as shown in Diagram 4, alternating ninepatch blocks with plain squares, and adding setting triangles and corner triangles to complete the rows. Sew the rows together to complete the quilt top.

FINISHING

Place the backing right side down on a flat surface. Place the batting and the quilt on top of the backing, right side up. Pin and baste the layers together. Quilt as desired. Bind as instructed on page 72.

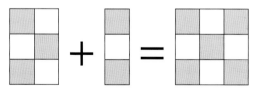

diagram 1 Combine two A units with one B unit to form the ninepatch block.

diagram 2 For the setting triangles, cut the squares on both diagonals to yield 44 triangles (two of these will be discarded).

diagram 3 For the corner triangles, cut two squares on one diagonal to yield 4 triangles.

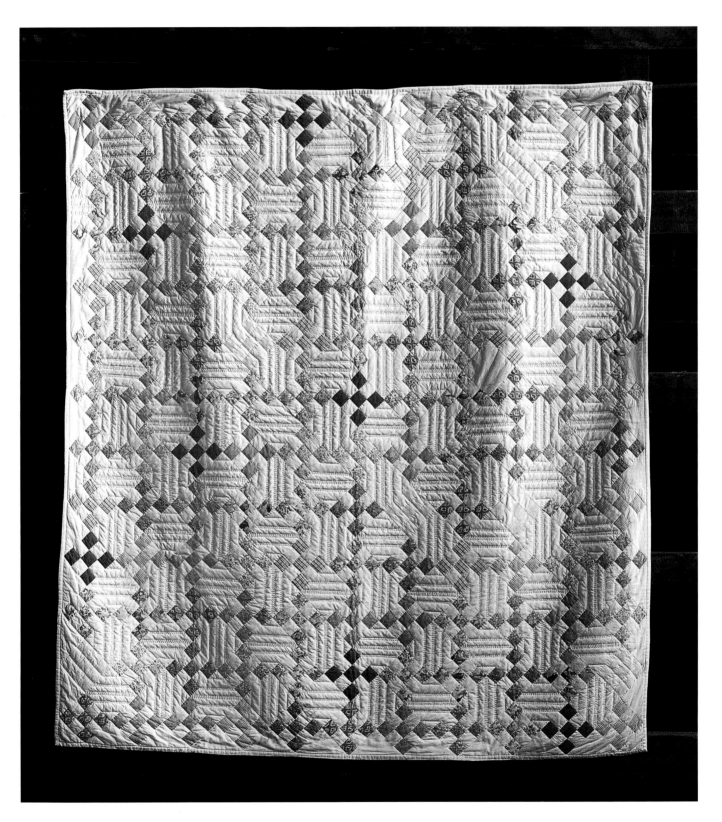

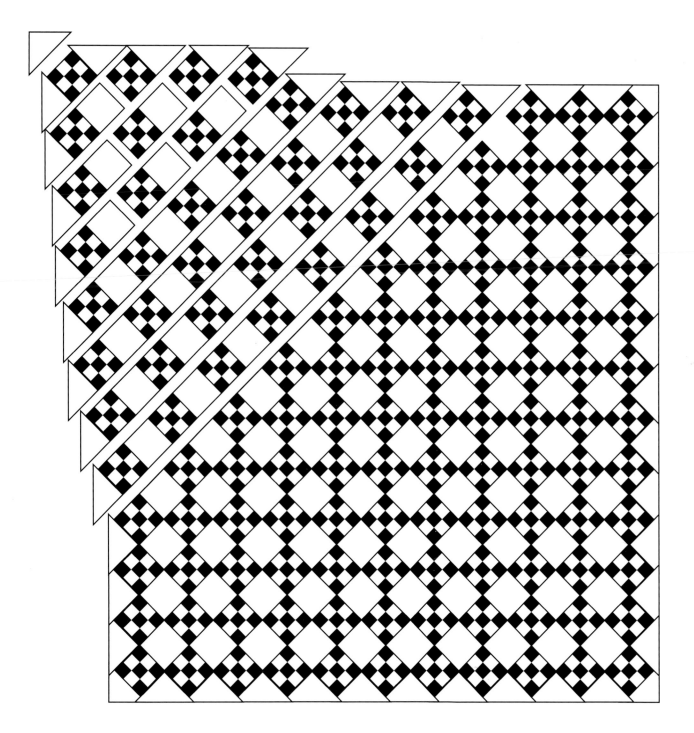

diagram 4 Quilt assembly: join the ninepatch blocks and cream squares into rows as shown, beginning and ending each row with a ninepatch block. Add the setting triangles to the end of each row and the corner triangles to the corners, then sew all the rows together to complete the quilt top.

Toile and ticking quilt

One of the simplest designs in this book, this quilt is within reach of anyone with even rudimentary sewing skills. Here, the plainness of ticking makes an effective contrast to the rococo qualities of the toile print. A black-and-white colour scheme keeps the look restrained.

Materials

2.5 m ticking, approx 56 in (140 cm) wide
2.5 m toile, at least 45 in (112 cm) wide
5.5 yd (5 m) black grosgrain ribbon, 5 cm
    (2 in) wide
For the backing: 5.5 yd (5 m) backing fabric,
    60 in (150 cm) wide; OR use a king-sized
    cotton bed sheet
Black sewing thread
White sewing thread
For the binding: 24 in (60 cm) black quilter's
    cotton, 45 in (112 cm) wide
King-sized thin batting
White quilting thread

Tools

Rotary cutter, ruler and mat
Sewing machine

Size

98 x 98 in (2.45 x 2.45 m)

Preparation

If your toile fabric is wider than 45 in (112 cm),
    trim it to size, centring motifs if necessary
    so that the panel is symmetrical

Seam allowance

Three-eighths inch (1 cm) seam allowances
    are used throughout

CONSTRUCTION

Quilt top Cut the ticking fabric in half lengthwise to give two pieces each 28 in (70 cm) wide. With right sides together and matching raw edges, join a piece of ticking to each edge of the toile panel. Using a ⅜ in (1 cm) seam, machine-sew in place using white thread in both the needle and bobbin. Cut the grosgrain ribbon in half widthwise. Centre a piece of ribbon along each seam between the ticking and toile panels, making sure it is straight, then machine-sew in place close to each edge of the ribbon, using black thread in the needle and white thread in the bobbin. See Diagram 1.

FINISHING

Join the backing fabric, if necessary. Press the seams open. Place the backing fabric face down on a flat surface. Place the batting and the quilt top on top of the backing, right side up. Pin and baste. Quilt by hand or machine as desired, firstly marking the quilting design lightly with tailor's chalk or pencil. Our example is hand-quilted lengthwise with large stitches down the centre of each motif in the toile fabric and also down every 7th or 8th white stripe in the ticking fabric, and is also machine-quilted (with black thread in the needle and white thread in the bobbin) along every 7th or 8th black stripe in the ticking, next to the hand-quilted white stripes. Alternatively, you could hand-quilt around the motifs in the toile.

BINDING

Across the width of the fabric, cut 9 strips each 2½ in (6 cm) wide. Join strips into a continuous length and bind quilt as described on page 23.

diagram 1 Quilt construction: the toile panel is flanked by strips of ticking. Wide grosgrain ribbon separates the panels. The quilt is finished with a mixture of hand- and machine-quilting.

Diamonds quilt

This lovely old-fashioned design is a showcase
for fabrics and a great way to use up scraps.
The dark panels use a myriad of colours and
prints. The border is easy to piece using extra
squares of colour. Use checked or solid-coloured
squares for a more masculine look.

Materials

All fabrics are 100% cotton, 45 in (112 cm) wide

For the squares: 2.8 yd (2.5 m) mixed
    fabrics. If buying fabric especially for this
    quilt, rather than using scraps, you will
    need 10 fat quarters or 20 fat eighths, or
    4 in (10 cm) of each of 25 different fabrics

For the background fabric and binding: 5 yd
    (4.5 m) seeded homespun

For the backing: 4.2 yd (3.8 m)

Batting at least 94 x 73 in (240 x 185 cm)

Tools

Rotary cutter, ruler and mat
Sewing machine

Size

86 x 65 in (220 x 185 cm)

Cutting directions

From the mixed fabrics, cut 266 squares each
    3½ x 3½ in (9 x 9 cm). You will need 102 for
    each of the panels of diagonal squares and
    the rest for the border. If you are using small
    fabric scraps, you will have to cut squares
    individually; if you are using larger scraps, fat
    quarters or fat eighths, you will be able to
    rotary-cut strips then cross-cut them into
    squares of the appropriate size

For cutting directions for the background
    fabric, see page 82

Seam allowance

Quarter-inch (6 mm) seam allowances
    are used throughout

Cutting directions for the background fabric

For the outer borders: from the length of the homespun fabric, cut two strips each 81¼ x 3 in (206.5 x 7.5 cm) for the side outer borders and two strips each 65 x 3 in (165 x 7.5 cm) for the top and bottom outer borders.

For the central background strip and inner borders: from the length of the homespun fabric, cut one strip 64¼ x 9 in (163.5 x 23 cm) for the centre panel. Cut two strips each 64¼ x 4¾ in (163.5 x 12 cm) for the side inner borders and two strips each 43 x 4¾ in (163.5 x 12 cm) for the top and bottom inner borders.

For the setting triangles: from the width of the remaining homespun fabric, cut 7 strips each 5½ in (14 cm) wide. Cross-cut these strips to yield fifty 5½ in (14 cm) squares. Cut each square again across both diagonals to yield 200 triangles.

For the corner triangles: from the width of the remaining fabric, cut 12 pieces each 3⅛ in (8 cm) square. Cut each across one diagonal to yield 24 triangles.

For the binding: from the width of the remaining fabric, cut 8 strips 2½ in (6 cm) wide.

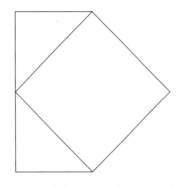

diagram 1: A units For the patterned border, sew a corner triangle to two sides of a plain square to make the A units. Make 8.

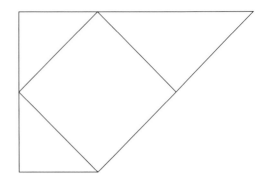

diagram 2: B units Sew a setting triangle to the top right edge of four of the A units to make B units.

CONSTRUCTION OF PANELS

On a flat surface, lay out the coloured squares, setting triangles and corner triangles, referring to Diagram 6. Move the coloured squares around until the overall effect is balanced. Ensure you divide the 102 coloured squares into 2 units each comprising 4 rows of 15 squares.
Sew the squares together into diagonal rows as shown in the diagram, adding the setting triangles and corner triangles as needed. Press the seams of each row in opposite directions. Sew the rows together, matching seams carefully. Press. Sew the second unit of coloured squares in the same manner. Sew a panel of coloured squares to either side of the plain centre panel. Press the seam toward the centre panel.

ADDING THE BORDERS

There are three borders: a plain inner border, a patterned border of coloured squares, and a plain outer border.

Plain inner border

Measure the length of the sewn squares through the centre rather than along the edge (as the bias edges of the setting triangles can stretch, distorting the edge of the quilt). Trim the centre cream strip and the two longer plain border strips exactly to this measurement. Attach the borders to

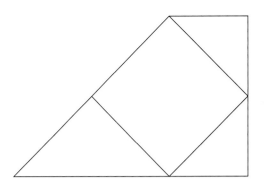

diagram 3: C units Rotate 4 of the A units 180 degrees. Sew a setting triangle to the bottom left edge of each of these units to make C units.

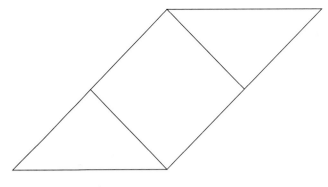

diagram 4: D units Sew the remaining setting triangles to the remaining plain squares to make 56 D units.

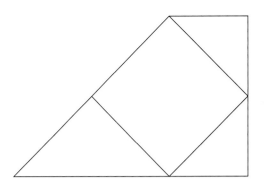

diagram 5: finished border Join the units as explained in the text to make the patterned borders.

the quilt centre, pinning at the midpoint and ends first, then along the length. Sew the border to each side of the quilt centre. Press. Measure the width of the quilt through the centre, including the side borders. Trim the two shorter plain border strips to this exact length and attach to the top and bottom of the quilt. Press.

Coloured border Sew a corner triangle to two sides of a plain square to make 8 A units (see Diagram 1). Sew a setting triangle to an A unit to make 4 B units (see Diagram 2) and 4 C units (see Diagram 3). Sew the remaining setting triangles to the remaining plain squares to make 56 D units

(see Diagram 4). For the top border, join 12 D units to make a row. Sew a B unit to one end of the row and a C unit to the other end (see Diagram 5). Repeat for the bottom border. For each of the side borders, join 19 D units. Sew a B unit unit to one end of the row and a C unit to the other end. Sew the 2 shorter patterned borders to the top and bottom of the quilt, then sew the 2 longer patterned rows to each side.

Plain outer border Sew the 2 longer outer border strips to the sides of the quilt. Sew the 2 shorter outer border strips to the top and bottom. Mitre the corners as explained on page 20.

Finishing

Quilt as desired. Our example has been hand-quilted with chevron designs between the squares in the patterned border and those on the edges of the two patterned panels. The direction of the chevrons is reversed at the midpoint of each side. The quilt has also been machine ditch-stitched in the seams of the squares.

For the binding, join the reserved binding strips into a continuous length and proceed as described on page 23.

diagram 6: quilt layout The two diamond-patterned panels adjoin a plain strip. A plain border surrounds the quilt centre. A patterned border made of coloured squares is then added, and finally a narrow plain outer border.

Pink silk button-tied quilt

This is an example of a tied quilt. Tying is an alternative to quilting as a means of finishing a quilt. It can be done with thread (either quilting or embroidery thread) or with buttons, as here.

The use of pretty flower-shaped buttons on pink silk results in an unapologetically girlie quilt, but using a darker or cotton fabric and plainer buttons would give a totally different effect.

Materials

All fabrics are 44 in (112 cm) wide

5½ yd (5 m) pink silk or silk-look polyester fabric for quilt top

4¾ yd (4.4 m) white silk or silk-look polyester fabric for quilt back

Pink sewing and quilting threads

White sewing thread

121 buttons (it is advisable to buy a few extra in case of future loss or breakage)

Thick polyester batting at least 94 x 94 in (240 x 240 cm)

Tools

Rotary cutter, ruler and mat

Sewing machine

Quilting hoop (optional)

Size

Approx 87 x 87 in (220 x 220 cm)

Cutting instructions

Ensure that the ends of both pieces of fabric are square.

From each piece of fabric, remove the selvages. From the width of the pink fabric, cut 9 strips each 2.5 in (6 cm) wide for the binding. Set aside.

Cut both pieces of fabric in half widthways. Leave one pink and one white piece whole to make centre panels for front and back respectively. Cut the other 2 pieces in half lengthways to make side panels for front and back respectively

Care instructions

Silk or polyester quilts, or those with expensive buttons, must be dry-cleaned. Cotton quilts with inexpensive plastic buttons can be hand-washed carefully

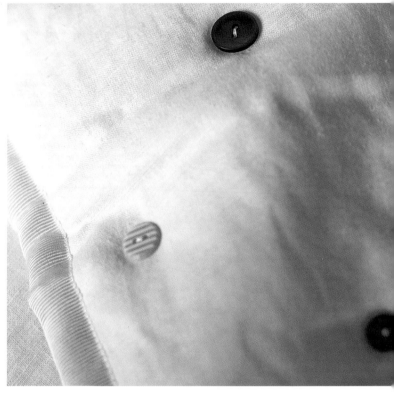

diagram 1: Quilt assembly Showing the seams along the centre panel and the placement of the buttons.

variation Quilt made with white cotton fabric and assorted buttons tied at rando points, then bound with white grosgrain ribbon.

Variation

This design also works well in a crisp cotton fabric or a warm wool or flannel. If you prefer a random look to a regimented grid pattern, sew on the buttons at irregular intervals, or use a selection of many different buttons as shown in the example above.

CONSTRUCTION

1 For the front, sew a side panel of pink fabric to each side of the centre front panel. Press seams open using a cool iron.

2 For the back, sew a side panel of white fabric to each side of the centre back panel. Press seams open using a cool iron.

3 Using a removable marker or tailor's chalk, mark the grid for the buttons on the quilt top, as shown in Diagram 1. To calculate the distance between the buttons, measure the distance between the panel seams and divide by 6. First, place evenly spaced marks down each front panel seam, then mark between and on either side of the panel seams.

4 Place the backing right side down on a flat surface. Place the batting and quilt top on top, right side up. Pin with safety pins.

5 Sew on buttons (this is most easily done with the fabric in a quilting frame) using quilting thread. Conceal the ends of the threads by running them into the wadding for 1 in (2.5 cm) or so, then bringing the needle up through the surface and cutting the thread off close to the surface.

6 Bind with reserved strips of pink fabric as described on page 23.

Stitch and slash quilt

The multiple layers of fabric used in this technique result in a wonderful dimensionality that mimics chenille. There is no need for batting in this quilt, as the layers give adequate weight. Machine-washing frays the cut edges of the fabric and adds to the chenille effect. The more you wash it, the softer the quilt will become.

Materials
All fabrics are 100% cotton, 44 in (112 cm) wide
For the centre of the quilt: 32 in (80 cm) of
    each of 5 different fabrics:
    For the front border: 28 in (70 cm)
For the back border: 28 in (70 cm)
Non-fusible interfacing such as Pellon:
    28 in (70 cm)
For the binding: 20 in (50 cm)

Tools
Rotary cutter, ruler and mat
Sewing machine

Size
Approx 41 x 53½ in (100 x 140 cm)

Seam allowance
Quarter-inch (6 mm) seam allowances are
    used throughout

step two Mark parallel diagonal lines ½ in (12 mm) apart on the right side of the fabric that will form the top of the quilt.

step six Sewing all lines in the same direction, machine-sew through all five layers along each of the marked lines.

Hints

The stich and slash method uses five layers of fabric. Narrow diagonal lines are sewn across the layers, then the top three layers are cut to form the chenille effect. The fourth layer is thus exposed and forms the background to the main fabric. The fifth fabric makes up the back of the quilt.

In our example, the fabric for Border 1 is the same as for the top of the quilt, and the fabric for the back border is the same as for the back of the quilt.

CONSTRUCTION OF CENTRE

1 Trim each of the 5 fabrics for the front of the quilt to 31½ x 44 in (80 x 112 cm).

2 Place the fabric for the front of the quilt on a flat surface, right side up. Press well. Using a quilters' ruler and an erasable marker or pencil, draw parallel diagonal lines ½ in (12 mm) apart. Draw the first line from corner to corner. To draw the remaining lines, align the ½ in marking on the edge of the ruler with the previous line.

3 Place the fifth fabric (the backing fabric) on a flat surface, right side down. Press well.

4 Layer the other 4 fabrics, right side up, on top of the fifth fabric, placing the marked piece for the front of the quilt on top. Align all raw edges. Press well.

5 Pin the five layers together to minimize fabric movement.

6 Wind the bobbin of your sewing machine with thread matching the bottom layer of fabric and thread your machine needle with thread matching the top layer of fabric. Stitch along each of the marked lines in the same direction using a stitch length of 3. (Note that sewing all the lines in the same direction will cause the fabric layers to

step seven Carefully cut through the top three layers only, leaving the bottom two layers intact.

Borders Sew the border fabrics and Pellon the the edges of the quilt.

move slightly out of alignment; do not worry about this, as the rectangle will be trimmed later to square it up.)

7 When all the stitching is completed, carefully cut through the top three layers of fabric (see the photograph), leaving the bottom two layers intact. This creates the chenille effect.

8 When all the cutting is completed, lay out the rectangle on a cutting mat and, using a rotary cutter, trim it to square up the edges, so that it measures approximately 29½ x 42 in (75 x 106.5 cm).

BORDERS

Measure both the length and width through the centre of the quilt.

Side borders These are cut 6½ in (16.5 cm) wide by the length of the quilt. Cut 2 from the front border fabric. Cut 2 from the back border fabric. Cut 2 of Pellon. Pin the back border pieces to the side edges of the back of the quilt, right sides together. Pin the front border pieces to the side edges of the front of the quilt, right sides together. Pin the Pellon on top of the front border. The order of components on each side edge of the quilt should be: back border, quilt, front border, Pellon.

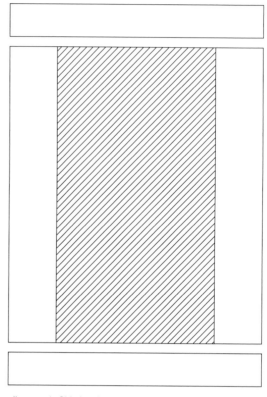

trimming borders Once the border pieces have been added, trim the ends if needed.

diagram 1 Side borders are sewn first to the central slashed panel, then the top and bottom borders are added.

Binding

From the width of the binding fabric, cut 5 strips each 2½ in (6 cm) wide. Seam the strips into a continuous length, making the joins at 45-degree angles, and proceed as described on page 23.

Stitch through all the layers on both edges. Fold the back border strips to the back of the quilt, the front border and Pellon strips to the front of the quilt, and press. Trim ends of borders if necessary. Pin the outer edge to hold the layers together.

Top and bottom borders These are cut 6½ in (16.5 cm) wide by the width of the quilt including the two side borders.
Cut 2 from the fabric for the front border.
Cut 2 from the fabric for the back border.
Cut 2 of Pellon.
Pin the back border pieces to the top and bottom edges of the back of the quilt, right sides together. Pin the front border pieces

to the top and bottom edges of the front of the quilt, right sides together. Pin the Pellon on top of the front border pieces. The order of components on the top and bottom edges should be as follows: back border, quilt, front border, Pellon.
Stitch through all the layers on both edges. Fold the back border strips to the back of the quilt, the front border and Pellon strips to the front of the quilt, and press. Trim the ends of the border if necessary. Pin the outer edge to hold the layers together.

FINISHING

Quilt a design in the border if desired.
Bind as decribed at left.

Ninepatch cot quilt

This bright and cheery cot quilt is quick and easy to make. The blocks are a variation on the traditional ninepatch design, with squares of printed fabric surrounding a plain centre.

Materials

All fabrics are 100% cotton, 44 in (112 cm) wide

For the coloured squares: a total of 32 in (80 cm) mixed scrap fabrics; or use 11 different fabric squares each 10½ x 10½ in (27 x 27 cm), or 11 strips each 44 x 2½ in (112 x 6 cm)

For the centre squares of the ninepatch, the sashing strips and the border: 1⅓ yd (1.2 m) white cotton

For the binding: 12 in (30 cm)

For the backing: 1.4 yd (1.2 m)

Tools

Rotary cutter, ruler and mat

Sewing machine

Size

Approx 44 x 36 in (112 x 90 cm)

Cutting directions

From the mixed scrap fabrics, cut 172 squares each 2½ x 2½ in (6 x 6 cm) for the coloured ninepatch squares. The squares may be rotary-cut or cut out individually using templates, as preferred

From the white cotton fabric:

For the central ninepatch squares, cut 20 squares 2½ x 2½ in (6 x 6 cm)

For the sashing strips, cut 7 strips each 2½ in (6 cm) wide across the width of the fabric, then cross-cut into 31 rectangles each 2½ x 6½ in (6 x 16.5 cm)

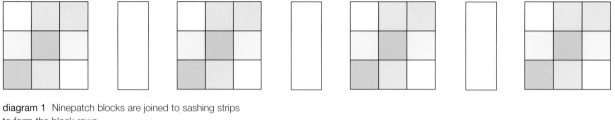

diagram 1 Ninepatch blocks are joined to sashing strips to form the block rows

diagram 2 Sashing strips are joined to 2½ in (6 cm) setting squares to form the sashing rows

diagram 3 The ninepatch block rows are alternated with sashing rows, then a border the same colour as the block centres and sashing strips is added.

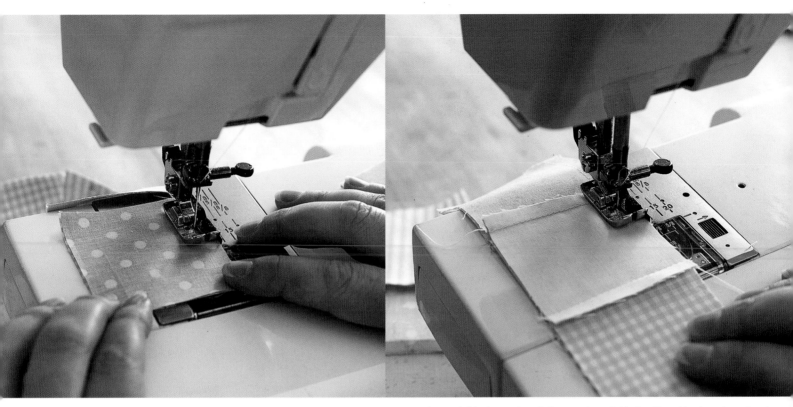

ninepatch blocks For the coloured strips, chain-piece pairs of coloured squares together, then add a single square to one end of each pair.

ninepatch blocks continued Sew a coloured strip to etiher side of a coloured-and-white strip to complete the ninepatch block.

CONSTRUCTION

Ninepatch blocks Each block consists of 8 coloured squares arranged around a white square (see Diagram 1). Piece the squares into strips first, then join the strips into blocks. Make sure there is a good range of prints in each block. Make 20 blocks.

ASSEMBLY

Block rows Sew 4 ninepatch blocks alternately with 3 sashing strips (see Diagram 1). Make a total of 5 block rows.

Sashing rows Sew 4 sashing strips alternately with 3 coloured setting squares. Make a total of 4 sashing rows.

Sew the block rows alternately with the sashing rows, beginning and ending with a block row, to complete the quilt centre.

BORDER

Find the length of the quilt by measuring vertically through the centre. From the white fabric, cut 2 strips each 3½ in (9 cm) by the length of the quilt (approx 38 in/ 96.5 cm). Sew in place and press.

Find the width of the quilt by measuring horizontally through the centre and including the two sewn side borders. Cut 2 strips each 3½ in (9 cm) by the width of the quilt (approx 36½ in/91 cm). Sew in place and press.

blocks The finished ninepatch block.

block rows and sashing rows Join blocks to sashing strips to form the block rows and coloured setting squares to sashing strips to form the sashing rows.

FINISHING

Place the backing right side down on a flat
surface and smooth it out. Place the batting
and the quilt on top of the backing, right
side up. Pin and baste the layers together.
Quilt as desired. The pictured example was
machine ditch-stitched in all the horizontal
and vertical seams.

BINDING

From the width of the binding fabric, cut
4 strips each 2½ in (6 cm) wide. Seam the
strips into a continuous length, making the
joins at 45-degree angles, and proceed as
decribed on page 23.

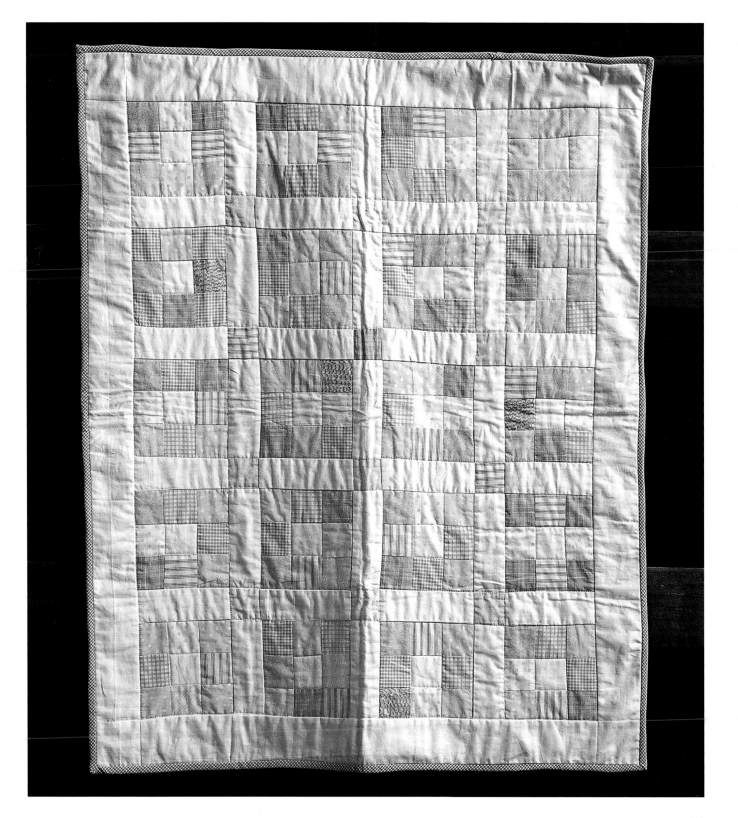

Folded Japanese quilt

This unusual folded quilt is surprisingly easy to make, as each block is simply a circle of fabric folded over a padded square, then quilted. This is a 'quilt-as-you-go' technique, meaning that batting and quilting are incorporated into each separate block, rather than being added once the quilt top is completed. For those who like the look of hand-quilting, but don't really enjoy the process, this technique breaks the task up into smaller, more manageable portions.

Materials

All fabrics are 100% cotton, 44 in (112 cm) wide

Mixed selection of Japanese indigo print
  fabrics to total 5.1 yd (4.6 m); for example,
  approx 18 fat quarters, or 9 in (25 cm) of
  each of 15 different fabrics

Mixed selection of cream print fabrics to total
  2 yd (1.7 m); for example, 81 squares each
  5¾ x 5¾ in (14.5 x 14.5 cm), or 12 in
  (30 cm) of each of 6 different fabrics, or 6 in
  (15 cm) of each of 12 different fabrics

For the border (optional): 1.6 m print fabric

For the binding: 16 in (40 cm) print fabric

Indigo sewing thread

Cream quilting thread

Thin cardboard for templates

Spray starch

Batting at least 70 x 70 in (175 x 175 cm)
  for quilt with border, or 60 x 60 in (155 x
  155 cm) for quilt without border

Tools

Rotary cutter, ruler and mat

Sewing machine

Size

Approx 60 x 60 in (155 x 155 cm) with border,
  52 x 52 in (132 x 132 cm) without border

Cutting directions for fabric

Notes: Before cutting the fabrics, prepare the
  templates (see page 104). Cut fabric on the
  straight of the grain wherever possible

For the circles: Place the 8½ in (21.5 cm)
  circle template onto the wrong side of the
  indigo fabric and cut out a circle by hand,
  leaving a good ¼ in (6 mm) turning
  allowance all the way round

For the cream centres and batting: Rotary-cut
  81 squares 5¾ x 5¾ in (14.5 x 14.5 cm)
  from both the cream fabric and the batting

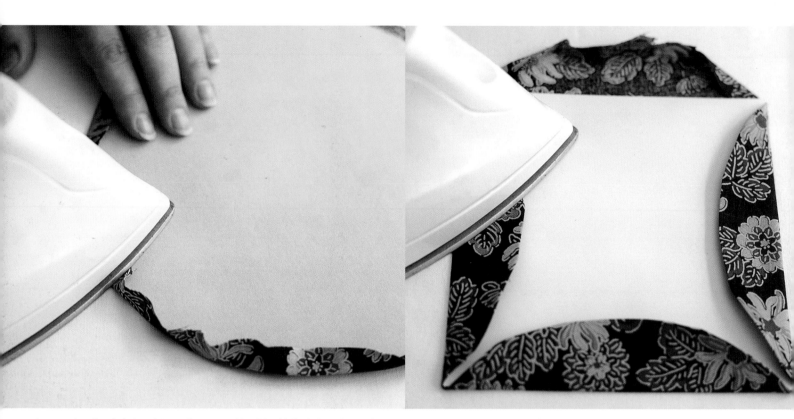

step one Lay the circle template on the wrong side of the fabric circle and press in the seam allowance over the template, using a dry iron.

step two Lay the 6 in (15 cm) square template over the centre of the fabric circle and press the edges of the fabric over the template.

Cutting directions for templates

From the thin cardboard, cut:
Circle 8½ in (21.5 cm) diameter
Square 6 x 6 in (15 x 15 cm)

Note: cut several of each, so that you have replacements for templates that become too worn or distorted.

CONSTRUCTION OF BLOCK

1 Spray the fabric circles with starch. Place the circle template in the centre of the wrong side of the fabric circle. Press in the seam allowance over the template using a dry iron (see photograph).

2 Lay the 6 in (15 cm) square template on the wrong side of the circle of fabric. Ensure that it is centred, and that the straight grain of the circle fabric aligns with the edge of the template. Fold the edges of the fabric circle over the template and dry press with a dry iron (see Diagram 1).

3 Open the flaps of the circle and replace the template with a square of wadding and a square of cream centre fabric.

4 Pin through the 4 layers using short appliqué pins. These permit you to stitch without catching the thread on each pin.

5 Using a small running sttich, quilt through all the layers approximately ⅛ in (3 mm) in from the edge (see photograph and Diagram 2). At each corner, make 3–4 small ladder stitches to bring the corner seams together. Make a total of 81 blocks.

step five Quilt through all the layers with an even running stitch.

assembly Join the finished blocks into rows by hand using a small ladder stitch.

ASSEMBLY

When you have completed quilting all the individual blocks, lay them out 9 across by 9 down, moving the blocks around to achieve a pleasing design. In our example, the blocks have been laid out alternating backs and fronts to give a reversible quilt. See Diagram 5 for an alternative layout. Join the blocks in each horizontal row, using a small ladder stitch. Then join the vertical rows in the same manner.

Border (optional) From the border fabric, cut 4 strips each 4½ x 54½ in (11 x 138.5 cm). Cut 4 strips each 4½ x 62½ in (11 x 160 cm).

From the batting, cut 2 strips 4½ x 54½ in (11 x 138.5 cm). Cut 2 strips each 4½ x 62½ in (11 x 160 cm).

With right sides together, pin a long strip of border fabric to one side of the front and back of the quilt. Place a strip of wadding on top and stitch ¼ in (6 mm) in from the raw edges. Trim evenly and press. Repeat for the other side, and then use the shorter strips for the top and bottom of the quilt.

BINDING

From the width of the binding fabric, cut 6 strips each 2½ in (6 cm) wide. Seam the strips into a continuous length, then proceed as described on page 23.

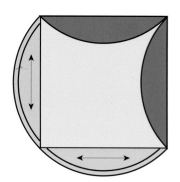

diagram 1 Align the straight grain of the fabric circle with the sides of the square template.

diagram 2 Quilt through all layers using a small running stitch.

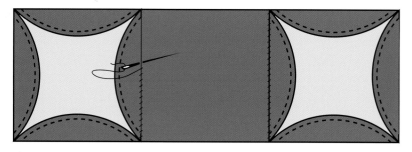

diagram 3 Join the finished squares into rows using a small ladder stitch.

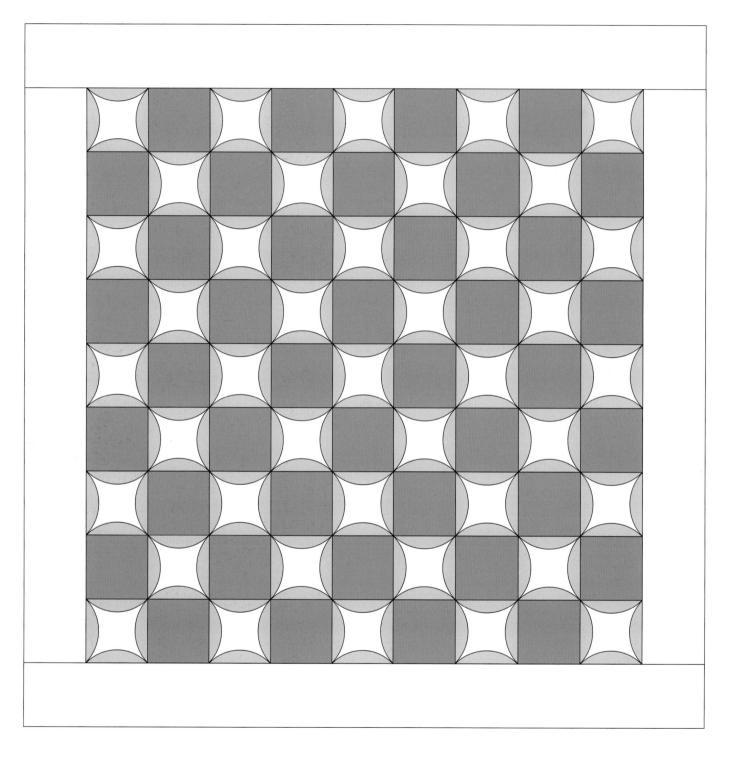

diagram 4 The blocks can be laid out so that they alternate back and front
to give a reversible quilt, as shown here, or as in Diagram 5.

diagram 5 This alternative layout shows the effect when all the blocks are arranged with their right sides up. This mimics a traditional pattern known as 'cathedral window', but is easier and quicker to achieve.

Index

Published in 2006 by Murdoch Books Pty Limited
www.murdochbooks.com.au

Murdoch Books Australia
Pier 8/9, 23 Hickson Road, Millers Point NSW 2000
Phone: +61 (0) 2 8220 2000   Fax: +61 (0) 2 8220 2558

Murdoch Books UK Limited
Erico House, 6th Floor North, 93–99 Upper Richmond Road, Putney, London SW15 2TG
Phone: +44 (0) 20 8785 5995   Fax: +44 (0) 20 8785 5985

Chief Executive: Juliet Rogers
Publisher: Kay Scarlett

Design concept: Tracy Loughlin
Art direction: Vivien Valk
Designer: Jacqueline Richards
Project manager and editor: Janine Flew
Photographer: Natasha Milne
Stylist: Sarah O'Brien
Diagrams and templates: Amanda McKittrick,
Heather Menzies, Jacqueline Richards
Production: Monika Paratore
Patterns: Penny Farnsworth and Ruth Van Haeff, Patches from the Past
Giant hexagon quilt (version on pages 8 and 41 made by Rae Gambrill), 1930s scrap quilt
(made by Penny Farnsworth), Square-in-a-square quilt, Scrappy ninepatch quilt,
Diamonds quilt, Stitch and slash quilt, Ninepatch cot quilt, Folded Japanese quilt.
Janine Flew: Silk and velvet log cabin quilt (made by Helen Henze),
Pleated silk quilt (quilted by Helen Henze), Raw-seamed denim and drill quilt,
Toile and ticking quilt (made by Helen Henze), Pink silk button-tied quilt (quilted by Alicia Barrios)

National Library of Australia Cataloguing-in-Publication Data
Van Haeff, Ruth. Quilt. Includes index
ISBN 9 78174045 7583. ISBN 1 74045 758 7
1. Quilting. I. Van Haeff, Ruth. II. Title. (Series : Handmade style). 746.46

Printed by 1010 Printing International Limited in 2006. PRINTED IN CHINA.

The Publisher and project designers also wish to thank Peter Brett and
Karen Hutchenson for their invaluable assistance in the production of this book.